VICARIUS ANIMÆ

SPECULATIVE I-STATEMENT IN JUNGIAN

PSYCHOTHERAPY

VICARIUS ANIMÆ

SPECULATIVE I-STATEMENT IN

JUNGIAN PSYCHOTHERAPY

Greg Mogenson

DUSK OWL BOOKS
London, Ontario, Canada

A title in the monograph series of
The International Society for Psychology as the Discipline of
Interiority, Vol. VIII

Published by
Dusk Owl Books
London, Ontario, Canada

Cover design and typesetting by
Michael Mendis

ISBN 978-1-7388606-0-9

CONTENTS

Part One

VICARIUS I-STATEMENT
FROM SUBSTANCE TO SUBJECT

PART TWO

SPECULATIVE INTERPRETATION
AND THE POETICS OF THE I

PART THREE

SOME FURTHER ASPECTS OF THE VICARIUS MEDIATION OF THE EXPERIENCE THAT CONSCIOUSNESS HAS HAD OF ITSELF

ACKNOWLEDGMENTS

A shorter version of Part One of this essay was presented at a conference of The International Society for Psychology as the Discipline of Interiority, which was dedicated to the theme of "The Soul's Logical Life" (July 7-11, 2021). The author is thankful for the encouraging response of the audience at that event, as well as to Pamela Power, Wolfgang Giegerich, Rita Mendis-Mogenson, and John Hoedl for their continuing collegial support all along the way.

SOURCES AND ABBREVIATIONS

The following abbreviations have been used for frequently cited sources:

CEP: Wolfgang Giegerich, *The Collected English Papers of Wolfgang Giegerich*, 6 vols., New Orleans: Spring Journal Books, 2005-2013. Cited by volume and page number. All volumes have been republished since 2020 by Routledge.

EL: G. W. F. Hegel, *The Encyclopaedia Logic. Part 1 of the encyclopaedia of philosophical sciences with zusätze*, trans. T. F. Geraets, W. A. Suchting, H.S. Harris. Indianapolis/Cambridge: Hackett Publishing Company, 1991. Cited by section and page number. Passages from additions to the text based on notes and transcriptions taken by attendees of Hegel's lectures will be indicated with the parenthesis: (as per the *Zusätze*).

PhS: G. W. F. Hegel, *Phenomenology of Spirit*, A. V. Miller, trans., Oxford: Oxford University Press, 1977 (original work published 1807). Cited by section and page numbers.

CW: Carl Gustav Jung, *Collected Works*, 20 vols. Herbert Read, Michael Fordham, Gerhard Adler and William McGuire, eds., R. F. C. Hull, trans., Princeton: Princeton University Press, 1957-1979. Cited by volume and paragraph number.

MDR: Carl Gustav Jung, *Memories, Dreams, Reflections*. Rev. ed., Aniela Jaffé. trans. Richard and Clara Winston. New York: Vintage Books, 1989, cited by page number.

Letters: Carl Gustav Jung, *Letters*. 2 vols. Ed. Gerhard Adler. Bollingen Series XCV: 2. Princeton: Princeton University Press, 1975.

Spring: *Spring: A Journal of Archetype and Culture*, New Orleans: Spring Journal Books. Cited by volume number, in some cases by year.

Part One

VICARIUS I-STATEMENT
FROM SUBSTANCE TO SUBJECT

> [...] lack[ing] ... a point which is distinct from
> [its] objects, [...] psychology inevitably merges
> with the psychic process itself. It can no longer be
> distinguished from the latter, and so turns into it.
> [...] the effect of this is that the process attains to
> consciousness. In this way, psychology actualizes
> the unconscious urge to consciousness. It is, in
> fact, the coming to consciousness of the psychic
> process, but it is not, in the deeper sense, an
> explanation of this process, for no explanation of
> the psychic can be anything other than the living
> process of the psyche itself.[1]
>
> —C. G. Jung

> [...] everything turns on grasping and expressing
> the True, not only as *Substance*, but equally as
> *Subject*.[2]
>
> —Hegel

The analyst's saying "I ..." on behalf of the patient

In *As You Like It*, through the mouthpiece of one of his characters, Shakespeare declares "the world's a stage [...] all [...] men and women merely Players."[3] Now, if this be so does

---

[1] Jung, *CW* 8 § 429.
[2] Hegel, *PhS*, § 17, p. 10.
[3] William Shakespeare, *As You Like It*, Act II, Scene vii, line 138.

it also mean that analysts, too, will be cast at times, not merely as one or another of the supporting characters of that familiar play called Transference, but at once both less than this and more, as the *understudies* or *stunt doubles* of the men and women who are their patients? I raise this question because of a mode of expression that I have become increasingly aware of using in my practice. In barest description, it amounts to this. After attentively listening to some matter of interest—be it a life situation or a dream, a symptom or an emotional experience—I am astonished to realize, "breaking a leg," as it were, that the interpretive comment I have then given voice to has the form of an I-statement said on behalf of the patient.

Now I hasten to emphasize that such utterances on my part, as effective and furthering as they typically are, have little or nothing to do with technique. I do not with artful intent set out to present my interpretations in this manner. Nor is it my intention, as I reflect in these pages upon this mode of expression, to put a new tool in anyone's toolkit. My interest, rather, is wholly limited to the phenomenality of such vicarius soliloquizing.[4] Out of the mouths of babes, analysts, and psychotherapists alike, my speaking in this way—both as the patient and for him—has phenomenon character. An event of meaning has occurred, in part, through my giving voice to it. Anticipating a bit, it could even be said that such statements as these are but the further determination of the materials being interpreted, the topics discussed—their becoming subject, as it were.[5] Which, of course, is pretty much what Jung was getting at

---

[4] *Vicarius*, the word used in the title of this essay (and here for the first time in the exposition itself), is not to be confused with the more familiar word vicarious, spelled with an o in it. For our purposes, the difference of meaning between these seemingly similar words may readily be expressed in terms of the psychological difference, "vicarius" being the term that refers to the vertical dimension or the soul side of the psychological difference, "vicarious" to the horizontal or ego side. Later, we will specifically discuss the meaning of the term in its traditional religious context.

[5] "Regardless of what topic or matter one's psychological work turns to, no matter what is to be studied psychologically […], in each case the whole point of the psychological work is to produce the psychological standpoint, the psychological I. This is the goal of the work[…]. Psychology does not aim for theoretical knowledge about the soul, for a kind of scientific doctrine, new information. The psychological standpoint or perspective is itself the *lapis* that it tries to reach." Wolfgang Giegerich, *What is Soul?*, (New Orleans: Spring Journal Books, 2012), p. 302.

with his essential insight that far from standing outside the psychic process as explanation of it, psychology is but the phenomenology-continuing *expression* of "the coming to consciousness of the psychic process" itself.[6] It only needs to be added that the same holds true for what the psychotherapist and analyst say. Their utterances, too, are not explanations of the patient's psychic situation or process, but rather and at best, the expression of "the coming to consciousness" of these.[7]

Simply, and yet not so simply, it happens like this. Concurrent with listening to the case material, there is a reflective moment in which listening gives way to what might be described as a thoughtful overhearing of itself restating what's been heard, and this, moreover, in such a way that, relating itself to itself in the matter at hand,[8] what I like to call the subject matter's I, gives rise to itself, voice to itself, as its own recursive and mercurial result.

Now, I say "the subject matter's I" to indicate occasions when the I that speaks is not the me that could be pointed at sitting vis-à-vis the patient in the consulting room, nor the patient, either, for that matter. While, of course, the two of us do sit there like that, speaking words for which we are separately responsible, the I that like some "third of the two" or "one for all" subsequently establishes itself,[9] far from existing beforehand, is only produced in the first place as the *mise-en-scène*-distilling result of its own saying— hence its characterization as the subject matter's I.

---

[6] Jung, *CW* 8 § 429. It is interesting to reflect Jung's denouncement of the naïve, straightforward idea of explanation in favour of an emphasis upon "the coming to consciousness of the psychic process" in the following line from Hegel: "The reason why 'explaining' affords so much self-satisfaction is just because in it consciousness is, so to speak, communing directly with itself, enjoying only itself; although it seems to be busy with something else, it is in fact occupied only with itself." Hegel, *PhS*, § 163, p. 101.

[7] Of course, below the niveau of a truly *psychological* psychology, psychologists do adapt a stance of external reflection and give explanations. But even then, the explanations provided are just as much an expression of the psychic process as the phenomena they are purported to be about.

[8] A resonance can be heard here to Kierkegaard's definition of the self as the relation that relates itself to itself.

[9] I say, "one for all" here to expand the sphere of reference of the more usual analytic term, "The Third of the Two."

But what does it mean, "produced as its own *mise-en-scène-*distilling result"? What kind of a subject is that? In the discussions that follow we shall be delving into this question. Here, at the outset, I would simply reply that just as one is not a listener before one listens or a interpreter before one interprets, so the subject is not truly that until, "breaking the fourth wall,"[10] so to speak, what can variously be called the concentrated result of the entirety of the material at hand, the distillate meaning of the setting and all the characters of the apperceptive surround, or again, the unity of the unity and difference of all the moments of the situation that has been "staged by the soul,"[11] has ventured to become conscious, ventured to say "I."

Objections and clarifications

A familiar saying has it that you never get a second chance to make a first impression. The counter-adage to this might be that nothing is really known until first impressions give way to second thoughts. Although I have only just introduced my topic, I suspect that initial impressions will have already brought some objections to the fore. First among these might be the very reasonable concern that analysts speaking in the manner I have described may be doing too much of the patients' work for them. In psychotherapy and analysis patients have to invest themselves, apply themselves. Different from medical and dental treatment, the talking cure depends upon their work, too. Wouldn't those times when the analyst stands in for the patient, saying "I …" on his or her behalf, undermine this requirement?

Another objection follows on the heels of this one. Would an analyst's speaking in this way not come across in a too authoritative manner? Analysts and therapists, after all, as Lacan aptly observed, are

---

[10] This terminological expression from the world of the theatre refers to occasions when an actor in a play breaks out of the scene he is in by speaking directly to the audience.

[11] Cf., Jung's reference to behaviours and happenings that are "merely staged, but staged in the peculiar way characteristic of hysteria, so that a *mise en scène* appears almost exactly like a reality." *CW* 4 § 364.

already in the position of "the one supposed to know."[12] Never mind that they may not know and may even be barking up the wrong tree. Surely, no licence should be issued for them to wildly act this out.

In response to these perfectly valid concerns, I can only reiterate what I said above about the phenomenon character of such interpretive statements. Far from being a technique that anyone should endeavor to apply, what I am here referring to as the analyst's speaking on behalf of the patient is just something that happens, if it happens at all. Having event character (or at least largely so), it is not authenticated by the analyst's authority, training, or skill, but only by its phenomenality as such. *Sozein ta phainomena.*

Another, this time more sympathetic, first impression might be that statements said on behalf of the patient constitute a form of empathy. Having felt into the patient, the analyst in this way demonstrates attunement with him. A chord has been struck in the resonance of which the rapport of the two edifies itself. Leston Havens speaks in this regard of "finding the patient,"[13] other practitioners of lending strength to the patient and "pulling him through" by inviting identification with the therapist. In response to this, I would only say that the kinds of statements I have in mind have less to do with empathizing with patients (as important as this may simultaneously be) than with opening-up the psychological difference.[14] Jung famously said it is not the psyche that is in us,

---

[12] "As soon as the subject who is supposed to know exists somewhere there is a transference." Jacques Lacan, *The Seminar. Book XI. The Four Fundamental Concepts of Psychoanalysis*, 1964, Alan Sheridan, trans. (London: Hogarth Press and Institute of Psycho-Analysis, 1977), p. 232.

[13] Leston Havens, *Making Contact: Uses of Language in Psychotherapy* (Cambridge, Massachusetts: Harvard University Press, 1986), pp. 11-26.

[14] Introduced into our literature by Wolfgang Giegerich, the psychological difference can be variously described as the difference between the psychic and the psychological, empirical contents and logical form, people and the concepts or consciousness that they exist as, ego and soul. Writes Giegerich: "True psychology depends on the awareness of what I call the 'psychological difference' (a kind of analogy to Heidegger's 'ontological difference'). It is the difference that runs through the meaning of the word psychology itself and divides 'psychology' as the account of the psychologies that people *have* (personalistic psychology) from 'psychology' as description of the life of the soul (which I claim beyond

but we who are in the psyche.[15] Whereas empathy is usually focussed upon the inner of the patient (upon his feelings and concerns at a personal or ego level), the vicarius I-statements that I have in mind are in each case the speculative or logic-speaking result of exposure to the entirety of the situation in which the (analyst as) patient finds himself.[16]

It is a matter, then, not of "vicarious introspection,"[17] as empathy has sometimes been called (though this may find a place in it, too), but of a gesture like the one Heidegger speaks of wherein the subject or interpreter takes a step back, as it were, to widen the horizon in front of him. The horizon widened in front of the interpreter—in our context, in front of the analyst in his role as the understudy or stand-in for the patient—corresponds to that second sense of psyche that Jung distinguished, the psyche we are in. While we may, to be sure, have plenty of subjective psychic content in our inner, the psyche that we are in and that surrounds us outwardly to the very horizon, has, as

---

Jung, is [...] a logical life in which we, as empirical personalities with our psychologies, live as in the invisible element or medium of our existence)." *The Soul's Logical Life,* pp. 123-124.

[15] "As I see it, the psyche is a world in which the ego is contained," Jung, *CW* 13 § 75. "You rightly emphasize that man in my view is enclosed in *the* psyche (not in *his* psyche)." 14 May 1950, Letter to Joseph Goldbrunner. Jung, *Letters,* Vol. 1., p. 556.

[16] The terms "speculative" and "speculation" in this essay are used in a sense analogous to their meaning within the context of the tradition of Speculative Philosophy (Kant, Fichte, Schelling, and especially Hegel). According to this tradition, concepts such as "soul," "truth," "love," "friendship," "freedom," and "justice," etc., are to be continuously measured against themselves in the situation at hand, which is also to say, defined and redefined via a rigorous process of immanent critique.

[17] Note here in this phrase the word "vicarious" and its difference from my references in this paper to "vicarius." Kohut, for whom empathy was of paramount importance, avers that the "idea of an inner life of man, and thus of a psychology of complex mental states, is unthinkable, without our ability to know via vicarious introspection—my definition of empathy." (Heinz Kohut, *The Restoration of the Self* [New York: International Universities Press, 1977], p. 306). "Vicarius," by contrast, is a Latin word meaning substitute or deputy and pertains to the mediating function that priests have on behalf of the faithful with respect to the sacred as well as to the full authority that Popes have as representatives of Christ on earth.

our dreams and apperceptions richly attest, the objective character and veracity of a scene or landscape, which of course is what Shakespeare was getting at when he said the world's a stage.

Analyzing from the Self

There is yet another first impression to be noted before delving any further into our topic. Or perhaps it would be better to speak, not of first impressions, in this case, but of an earlier conceptualization, since here we have to do with an already-existing psychological formulation that would readily claim the phenomenon I have described as an instance of itself.

In the Jungian tradition a distinction is drawn between "analyzing from the Self," on the one hand, and analyzing from the persona and the ego, respectively, on the other. In an insightful essay on this topic, John Haule presents a number of anecdotes concerning Jung's remarkable facility with respect to the first-mentioned of these modes of interpretation. One of these, a recollection of Marvin Spiegelman, is from a final meeting that he as newly fledged analyst had had with Jung just after graduating from the Jung Institute. Following upon an initial period of sitting together, with it seemed nothing to say to each other, Jung, reports Spiegelman,

> began to speak, from out of himself somewhere. He spoke of his own life. Throughout all this apparent soliloquy, I was totally present too and I had the experience, subsequently reported by others also, that Jung was "speaking to my condition," and addressing himself to all my problems, fears, concerns, and deep desires. Most of all, it was an experience of Self speaking to Self.[18]

Another example of Jung analyzing from the Self is recounted by Jane Wheelwright, who had sessions with him in the 1930s. In her

---

[18] Cited by John Haule, "Analyzing from the Self: an empirical phenomenology of the 'third' in analysis" in Roger Brooke, editor, *Pathways into the Jungian World: Phenomenology and Jungian Psychology* (London, New York: Routledge, 2000), p. 257.

report Wheelwright speaks of how in Jung's presence "one felt as though all the surrounding matter had turned into whirling molecules." Continuing, she states,

> Everything there seemed to be moving, melting, changing forms. Everything stirred. Reality blurred, conversation happened unplanned. I felt someone, not me, spoke through me and someone not Jung was speaking through him. There was also the feeling of being swept into the depths of a perilous, dangerous underworld but since Jung had descended into this strange world and emerged so could I. In his presence I did not register on the difference of our statures! An archetype had taken over? Whatever it was, it seemed to be creating before my eyes and ears and senses, a model of the changed person I was meant finally to become. Trying the new me on, so to speak. Equally strange was Jung. Instead of being the doctor who cures you, he was allowing himself to be equally affected [...] Two people were caught in a vise that was forcing them to undergo an important rearrangement of themselves that had significance—some meaning far beyond them.[19]

Although in neither of these recollections is Jung described as overtly saying "I" on behalf of the patient, there is much in them that is in accord with the account I have given thus far of the analyst's voicing interpretations in this way. Spiegelman characterizes Jung as delivering an "apparent soliloquy" in which "I was totally present too ..." Jung, he said, "spoke of his [Jung's] own life," but this in a manner that fully addressed Spiegelman's "problems, fears, concerns, and deep desires." Wheelwright, for her part, in describing her exchanges with Jung, also emphasizes a dissolving of personal boundaries between herself and Jung. As she puts it in the passage quoted, "In his presence I did not register on the difference in our statures!" "I felt someone, not me, spoke through me and someone not Jung was speaking through him."[20]

---

[19] *Ibid.*, p. 258. The word "vice" in the original is corrected here to read "vise."
[20] Here is a nice example of "the third of the two."

No doubt, what is here described by these former analysands of Jung is quite in keeping with the kind of interpretive statements I am concerned with in this essay. Having served them in the role of *vicarius animae* (if I may already use this term in advance of presenting its meaning more fully below), Jung is remembered as having given voice to their soul situation, and this, moreover, not from some doctorly perch outside, but in the manner of an intercessor, from out of their own depths. The only problem with these accounts is that without any discussion of the actual analytic work that was conducted or of the truths discussed, they amount to little more than idealizing tributes to Jung as intuitively gifted analyst and mana-personality, on the one hand, and to the archetype of the Self, on the other.

Now it is true, of course, that Jung was a great man and master analyst. What is pertinent in our context, however, has more to do with the analyst's putting off *his* greatness, *his* brilliance, and letting the material at hand—in these cases, the soul situation of his patients—speak through him.[21] Though not explicitly indicated in these reports, this, I suspect, was very much at play in Jung's work as an analyst. Just as Mrs. Wheelwright recalls that she did not register the difference of stature between herself as Jung's patient and he as her doctor, neither, evidently, did Jung. On the contrary, his speaking as and for the patient was rooted in his having truly taken that old adage of the Latin dramatist Terence to heart, the one about nothing human being alien to me. And it follows from this that the speculative insight that the Jungian tradition has formulated as "analyzing from the Self" is more humbly sourced than its usual, more idealized conceptualization suggests. For, indeed, as Jung characterizing this essential aspect of his analytic attitude once put it, "As a medical psychologist I do not merely assume, but I am thoroughly convinced that *nil humanum a me alienum esse* is even my duty."[22] That Jung fulfilled this duty in Mrs. Wheelwright's case is

---

[21] On this point compare Hegel's statement: "When I think, I give up my subjective particularity, sink myself in the matter, let thought follow its own course; and I think badly whenever I add something of my own." Hegel (as per the *Zusätze*), *EL* § 24, p. 58.

[22] Letter to Herbert Read 2 Sept. 1960, Jung, *Letters* 2, p. 589.

evident from her statement, "Instead of being the doctor who cures you, [Dr. Jung] was allowing himself to be equally affected […]."[23]

But, of course, there are other, less humble cherries in the bowl besides this one. When Jungian tradition speaks of analyzing from the Self it usually has something much grander in mind. Consider, for example, the following passage from Jung's essay, "Basic Postulates of Analytical Psychology":

> If it were possible to personify the unconscious, we might think of it as a collective human being combining the characteristics of both sexes, transcending youth and age, birth and death, and, from having at its command a human experience of one or two million years, practically immortal. If such a being existed, it would be exalted above all temporal change; the present would mean neither more nor less to it than any year in the hundredth millennium before Christ; it would be a dreamer of age-old dreams and, owing to its limitless experience, an incomparable prognosticator. It would have lived countless times over again the life of the individual, the family, the tribe, and the nation, and it would possess a living sense of the rhythm of growth, flowering, and decay.[24]

Now the point of criticism that I want to bring to this, once again, in other respects wonderful passage, has to do with the idealized conception of the Self it implies. Jung begins by entertaining the possibility of *personifying* the unconscious. And a sentence later he adds the phrase, "if this being existed ..." Well, of course, it is possible to personify the unconscious. Jungian psychology's concept of the Self does that, at least in the way it is commonly referenced and commonly used.[25] As for conceiving of "*the* unconscious" as an

---

[23] Taking this a step further, we can surmise that being "equally affected" was an important part of how Dr. Jung facilitated the cure.

[24] Jung, CW 8 § 673. This passage might alternatively be read, not in terms of Jung's phrase, "if this being existed," but as a description of the infinitely negative speculative subject or logical I (about which more later).

[25] Although in the passage cited Jung speaks of "the unconscious" (note here his use of the hypostasizing definite article), his description of it as a *coincidentia*

existing being—well once again, the concept of the Self does that, too. But here we need to see that analyzing from the Self as thusly conceived is very different from the analyst's speaking as the I of the patient's situation. As conceived of by Jung, the unconscious that the Self supposedly draws upon and personifies (and that the analyst when analyzing from the Self speaks from) is as timeless as it is primordial. Which is why the speech that it gives rise to (this is one way of characterizing the tributes to Jung that we heard) tends to the oracular. The I, by contrast, exists in time, it is a thoroughly historical product. By this I mean that it has, or rather, *is* its moment, and lasts only as long as its moment lasts. Far from being oracular, the speech which manifests as I is completely bound to its time and place, so much so, in fact, that it is nothing else than the inwardness of these, which is also to say, the subjectivity and truth of the situation in play or matter at hand.

From here we can return to my earlier having characterized the I-statements that the analyst makes on behalf of the patient as being the *result* of a reflective psychic process, its coming to consciousness, as it were. In contrast to this, what the Jungian tradition conceptualizes as analyzing from the Self implies an already existing subject behind subjectivity. Further to, or as a function of, the metapsychological set-up to which much of Jungian psychology has succumbed,[26] we have when thinking in these terms, not the self-constituting I that is of interest to us in these pages, but an external relation between two its—the posited-as-already-existing ego, on the one hand, and the posited-as-already-existing archetype of the Self, on the other. The problem with this, however, is that conceived of in these terms, subjectivity does not have subject character. It is an object, an it, an ego, a Self, or the relation between these thing-like figures. Not subject in the sense of logic-expressing voice of the situation. Not subject in the sense of I.

---

oppositorum ("combining the characteristics of both sexes, transcending young and age, birth and death") describes as well the Self of his theorizing.

[26] It is important to realize that the term "metapsychology" is a misnomer. For a truly *psychological* psychology there is no meta-level outside the soul to theorize from and, thus, no such thing as metapsychology.

In lieu of an example

I can well imagine that an example would be appreciated at this point, a clinical vignette or verbatim report, perhaps. I find, however, that I am unable to provide anything of the sort. It is not that I cannot recall the content of pertinent sessions or remember how this content was discussed. It's that as soon I try to attribute to myself the statements I've made when speaking as and for the patient at a soul level, they become immediately indefinite and slip away, like dreams forgotten upon waking. When first I noticed this, I found it discouraging. Could this topic even be written about, such being the case? But then I realized, tarrying with the negativity of this, that this peculiarity is not a fault, but belongs to the character of the phenomenon itself. What is said on behalf of the patient as an I-statement (by the analyst in the first person vicarius!) is not a content that can be isolated out from the situation that gave rise to it. For higher or deeper than that, such statements are the situation of interest or matter at hand's insightfully giving voice to the logical movement and conceptual unity of its constituent aspects, and this, moreover, in the less literal, and more universalized manner of the form of subject.

Now some I am sure upon hearing this phrase, "form of subject," will be put in mind of the "I think" of Descartes' famous cogito or of the "I-think" as it is conceived of in the philosophy of Kant. These logical touchstones of our philosophical tradition, however, present the subject in terms of the ordinarily prevailing conception which thinks in terms of an external relation between a knowing subject, on the one hand, and an object to be known, on the other. In them an abstractly subjective I, which is held to be the ground of certainty or agent of apperception, is conceived of as standing outside and prior to an external world of things which it subsequently casts into its own representational terms and thinks determinate thoughts about. But this, as I just called it, abstract subjectivity, ill-accords with the insight of Jung's that was discussed above in which psychology is characterized, less as an explanation of the psyche from without, than as a phenomenology-continuing expression of the soul's making itself, becoming conscious of itself, and giving voice to itself in some real and pressing situation that is at the same time indicative of it, its reified expression. For a better fit with respect to this, let us call it, soulful or psychological I, it is rather to Hegel's insights concerning the absolute subjectivity of an I that is as at home with itself on the object side of the ordinarily prevailing difference of consciousness as it is on the subject side to which we should turn.[27] But before we delve into this, I would first like to offer, in lieu of the example I am unable to provide, some commentary on a text of Jung's that readily lends itself as an ersatz for this.

In his essay, "Individual Dream Symbolism in Relation to Alchemy,"[28] Jung provides an extensive commentary on the dream series of a dreamer about whom little more is indicated than that he was "a young man of excellent scientific education."[29] Now the odd, but in our context, interesting thing about this commentary is that it is adduced by Jung in a completely vicarius manner. Or perhaps, it would be better to say, in an *absolutely* vicarius manner, since the commentary and interpretations that Jung offers are absolute in the sense of their being *absolved* (= freed) from the difference between the dreamer and the analyst. The circumstance of this was that Jung did not want to influence the production and content of the dreams with his presence and so did not take the dreamer on as his patient. It was only after the dreams of this series were dreamt that Jung became their analyst. And how, it may be wondered, did he manage this—to interpret the dreams without the dreamer to provide them with context and associations? As questionable as this may be to some, Jung met this challenge by taking the series itself as the context of each particular dream and then "proceed[ing]," as he put

---

[27] Though both Kant and Hegel belong to the tradition of speculative philosophy, they differed in that while Kant offered a subjective idealism that was steeped in epistemological concerns, Hegel offered an absolute idealism, that is, an idealism that was "absolved" from the subject/object difference as ordinarily conceived.

[28] Jung, *CW* 12, pp. 39-223.

[29] *Ibid.*, § 45.

it, "as if I had had the dreams myself and were thereby in a position to supply the context."[30]

Turning now to a dream of this series, let us observe as best we can its being interpretatively changed-up into the form of subject by the analyst's saying I in the patient's stead, or as Jung just worded this, by his approaching the dream as if he had dreamt it himself.

The twelfth dream of the dream series is presented in a single sentence:

> *The dreamer finds himself with his father, mother, and sister in a very dangerous situation on the platform of a tram-car.*[31]

Interiorizing himself into this dream, debuting upon its stage as if he were its dreamer, Jung declares with respect to the figure of the dreamer,

> He has fallen right back into childhood, a time when we are still a long way from wholeness. Wholeness is represented by the family, and its components are still projected upon the members of the family and personified by them. But this state is dangerous to the adult because regressive: It denotes a splitting of the personality which primitive man experiences as the perilous "loss of soul." In the break-up the personal components that have been integrated with such pains are once more sucked into the outside world. The individual loses his guilt and exchanges it for infantile innocence; once more he can blame the wicked father for this and the unloving mother for that, and all the time he is caught in this inescapable causal

---

[30] Jung, *CW* 12 § 49. Another example of Jung's proceeding in this manner occurs in the context of his interpretations of the Miller fantasies. After expressing regret that more information was not known about the cause of Miss Miller's worry and anxiety during a particular period, he offers the following consolation: "Maybe this lack has its advantages, in that our interest in the general validity of the fantasy now struggling to be born is not obscured by any sympathetic concern for the personal fate of the author. This obviates the difficulty which often prevents the doctor, in his daily work, from turning his eyes away from the wearisome mass of petty detail to the wider relationships where every neurotic conflict is seen to be part of human fate as a whole" *CW* 5 § 252.

[31] Jung, *CW* 12 § 151.

nexus like a fly in a spider's web, without noticing that he has lost his moral freedom. But no matter how much the parents and grandparents have sinned against the child, the man who is really adult will accept these sins as his own condition which has to be reckoned with. Only a fool is interested in other people's guilt, since he cannot alter it. The wise man learns only from his own guilt.[32]

There is a further sentence that follows upon this that I shall turn to in a moment. In it, as we shall see, the foregoing passage culminates in a more forthright approximation of the analyst's speaking as the patient's I. Before citing this, however, a few words about the interpretation thus far. Although we can surely take Jung at his word that when he says that he has taken up each dream in the series as if he had dreamt it himself, it is also the case that his commentary as it is given up to this point comes across in a more external manner than his adoption of such a methodological conceit would have led us to expect. That this is so may be attributed to Jung approaching the dreams of the series with the aim of demonstrating that the concept of wholeness and the motif of the mandala may be discerned across them. From outside the dreams, he brings this already existing theoretical interest to bear upon them.[33] And to this I would add that his commentary also lapses into externality due to his referring to the dreamer (whose dreams he is interpreting as if he had dreamt them himself) in the

---

[32] *Ibid.,* § 152.

[33] When we relieve the dream of Jung's purpose of using it to exhibit the inception and development of mandala symbolism in the individuation process, it becomes apparent that his interest in this topic amounts to what might be called a regressive externalization of the stance of interiority that had already been achieved with his great insight into psychology's lack of an objective, or extra-psychic, Archimedean point. For compared to the methodological standpoint that is rooted in this truly psychological insight, the mandala, at least as it has been appropriated by Jung, stands in something of the same relation as did the Golden Calf to the Tablets of the Law. Psychology, however, does not need to see mandalas in front of itself. The dialectical mode of interpretation that follows from the insight into the Archimedeanlessness of psychology is already uroboric, already a circular wholeness able to reflect its subject matters into themselves, releasing thereby what they have to say about the soul.

third person. But let us set aside these (from our point of view) inconsistencies, the better to appreciate the interpretive power of the more speculative utterance with which Jung ends this paragraph. Immediately following upon the last line that I quoted, the one where it is stated that "The wise man learns only from his own guilt," Jung adds that such a one will rather ask himself, "'Who am I that all this should happen to me?'," even as he looks into his own heart for the answer.[34]—A fair approximation, this, of what I am calling vicarius I-statement.

Now, of course, if the dreamer had been Jung's patient and this dream had been presented in an actual session, it would have been given in the first person, not the third. It would have read, *"I find myself with my father, mother, and sister in a very dangerous situation on the platform of a tram-car."* With this in mind, we can readily imagine how a more fulsome speculative interpretation could have unfolded. Just by restating the dream out loud, the analyst would become the speaker of its I. More boldly than the patient, perhaps, who most often cannot make head nor tail of his dreams, the analyst would then proceed to read and re-read it in a way that lets all the details that are predicated of the I come home to the I, even as, maintaining itself in the face of such self-othering negations, the I constitutes itself in the first place as their sublated result.

"I've fallen right back into my childhood," declares the analyst into the room, after restating the dream verbatim in the first person. "I'm with my family in a dangerous situation, dangerous because regressive," he then vicariusly continues. "The integrated, self-responsible man that I am, has unravelled into mother, father, and sister." "But while this is so," we can imagine him then saying, "I do not succumb, but rather ask myself" (and with these words the aforementioned "fourth wall" is broken such that, applying itself to itself, consciousness becomes self-consciousness): "Who am I that all this should happen to me?"

---

[34] Jung, *CW* 12 § 152.

The speculative subjectivity of the self-positing I

In the question Jung gave voice to on behalf of the dreamer, a speculative form of the I posits itself, establishes itself. By this I mean that the I referred to by Jung in his vicarius I-statement is not so much some already existing ego to which things have additionally happened, but the other way around, the result in the first place of the names it gives to the circumstances and contingencies that it sublatedly produces itself as the logical essence or knower of.

Now with this name-conferring, subjectivity-constituting turning of the tables upon circumstance and contingency in mind, let us take up my earlier claim that it is to Hegel we should turn for insight "concerning the absolute subjectivity of an I that is as at home with itself on the object side of the ordinarily prevailing difference of consciousness as it is on the subject side."[35] The first thing to be noted with respect to this is that while "I" is simply a pronoun that designates the unique subjectivity of the me that each of us are, it is also and at the same time a universal that, in what might be called an "it takes one to know one" manner, produces itself as the knower of other universals and of universality as such.

Universals, of course, are the substance of things, the essence through which they are what they are. We could also say that universals are that which remains the same in something even while that something is subject to change—its definition, its concept, its name. Closest to us in this respect is our own universality as I. Throughout all the changes and negations that we happen to go through there is an intelligible essentiality, unseen by the senses, that becomes conscious of itself as consciousness, conscious of itself as

---

[35] Cf. "In the Logic, thoughts are grasped in such a way that they have no content other than one that belongs to thinking itself, and is brought forth by thinking. So these thoughts are *pure* thoughts. Spirit is here purely at home with itself, and thereby free, for that is what freedom is: being at home with oneself in one's other, depending upon oneself, and being one's own determinant." Hegel (as per the *Zusätze*), *EL* § 24, p. 58.

I, by sublating the vicissitudes that we are subject to, even as at the same time, distinguishing itself from itself in the same stroke as it distinguishes itself from all that it is not, it comes to know, to be the knower of, the essentiality or truth of everything else.

Writing with respect to the first part of this insight, Hegel states that "When I say 'I,' I mean myself as this singular, quite determinate person, but when I say 'I,' I do not in fact express anything particular about myself. Anyone else is also 'I,' and although in calling myself 'I,' I certainly mean me, this single [person], what I say is still something completely universal."[36] As for the second part of the insight, the part about the I as the universal that knows other universals, apropos of this, Hegel speaks in the line above the one I just quoted of how, in contrast to animals (which see what they see, their food for example, only as singular things), "man reduplicates himself in such a way that he is the universal that is [present] *for the universal*," adding that "This is the case for the first time when man knows himself as an 'I.'"[37]

But how, it might be asked, is this reduplication achieved? And how is it that man, or in our context, the patient, comes to know himself thereby as I?

We just heard from Hegel about the simultaneity of the two senses of I. When we point at ourselves and say "me" (or "I" in the sense of "me") reference is made to a particular, highly-limited determination of subjectivity. This limited determination of subjectivity, however, may readily turn into the opposite of itself, for when finitude is acknowledged, limits known, a dialectic may come into play wherein these are exceeded, the self-identicalness of the subject transcended. "The animal or the stone," writes Hegel, "know nothing of its limit. In contrast, the I, as knowing or thinking in general, is limited but knows about the limit, and in this very knowledge the limit is only a limit, only something negative outside

---

[36] *Ibid.*, p. 57.
[37] *Ibid.*

us, and I am beyond it."[38]—Why it is quite as if, having wrestled with the limits that mediate its negation as with an angel, consciousness becomes self-consciousness, this being the blessing it thereby receives. And it is owing to this, to its having become conscious of itself as consciousness, that the I "as knowing and thinking in general" can interiorize other phenomena into the limits within which they are inscribed, discerning thereby the character of situations and essence of things, much as Adam did in Eden when he gave the animals their names.

The point to be grasped is that the limits dialectic that is constitutive of consciousness having become self-conscious is the same as the reduplication dialectic wherein thinking or the I meets its non-identity with itself (i.e., its infinity as negative) in whatever it is limited by, which is also to say, as the mediated surplus of all that it is not.[39] As Hegel in a passage that squares nicely with the reference that I just made to Adam naming the animals in Eden puts it,

> In thinking an object, I make it into thought and deprive it of its sensuous aspect; I make it into something which is directly and essentially mine. Since it is in thought that I am first by myself, I do not penetrate an object until I understand it; it then ceases to stand over against me and I have taken from it the character of its own which it had in opposition to me. Just as Adam said to Eve:

---

[38] G.W. F. Hegel, *Lectures on the Philosophy of Religion, One-Volume Edition. The Lectures of 1827*, Peter C. Hodgson, editor, R. R. Brown, P. C. Hodgson, and J. M. Stewart, trans. (Berkeley, Los Angeles, London: University of California Press, 1988), p. 173.

[39] Hegel's point (about how when consciousness comes to know about its limit it to that extent transcends it) invites comparison to a statement of Jung's: "What I call transformation is at bottom a question of fate. Although we may wish to keep within our limits, or to overstep them, it is never done by wishing but only by happening. Only when it happens to us that we overstep our limits can we be sure that we have overstepped them and that it had to be so. In the end there is no legitimate having-to-go-beyond-ourselves. Hence I would not recommend anybody to wish to go beyond himself. Moreover this expression is false; we cannot go beyond ourselves but only deeper into ourselves, and this self is not identical with the ego *because in this self we appear wondrously strange to ourselves.*" To Ewald Jung, 31 July 1935, *Letters*, vol. I, p. 193. My italics.

'Thou art flesh of my flesh and bone of my bone', so mind says: 'This is mind of my mind and its foreign character has disappeared.'[40]

This is an important statement. Updating that great speculative Ur-statement of the bible, "flesh of my flesh and bone of my bone,"[41] and surpassing as he does so the limit that his predecessor, Kant, had seemed to impose upon knowing, the cognitively more ardent Hegel vividly conveys the difference-sublating "intentionality toward the other"[42] through which the logic that pervades both the subject side and the object side of the ordinarily prevailing difference of consciousness—let us call this, the rib that these both share! [43]—gives voice to itself as I. And here it may be added that it is this I, which in another context Hegel has characterized as "an 'I' that is a 'We' and a 'We' that is an 'I',"[44] that the analyst gives voice to on those vicariusly interpretive occasions we are concerned with in this paper, "mind of my mind," indeed.

Variations on this theme from Jung and Giegerich

A moment ago, I referred to our text from Hegel as an updating of the great sentence from the bible that he had cited in it. Updating again, several other passages come to mind, one from Jung and a couple more from Giegerich. In the first of these, Jung, in the course of speaking to students of the Jung institute about the interpretation of dreams, encourages them to expose themselves wholeheartedly to the material at hand, interpreting it boldly. The analyst, he declares, "must give credit to his own interpretation. He must have courage, he must help; [otherwise] it is as if a man is

---

[40] G. W. F. Hegel, *Hegel's Philosophy of Right*, T. M. Knox, trans. (London, Oxford, New York: Oxford University Press, 1976), p. 226. The passage is from the "Additions" appendix. Such additions are based on notes and transcriptions taken by attendees of Hegel's lectures on the topic discussed.

[41] *Genesis* 2:23.

[42] Giegerich, *The Soul's Logical Life*, p. 204.

[43] The allusion is to the rib of Adam from which Eve was made.

[44] Hegel, *PhS*, § 177, p. 110.

bleeding to death and you *ponder!*"⁴⁵ Reading these words we may be reminded of the descriptions Marvin Spiegelman and Jane Wheelwright gave of Jung's work with them in analysis. Clearly, when offering interpretations to his patients, Jung shared a rib with them, in the sense of this described. As for Jung's own further account of the interpretive boldness he recommends, this he maintains can be confidently ventured to the extent that the analyst is at the same time modest enough to take correction from the further unfolding of the psychic process. "You can only say, 'My God, I don't *know*, but if it is an error, the unconscious will correct it.'"⁴⁶ It is by being faithfully rooted in such a conviction, at the same time as he is immersed in the matter at hand, that the analyst is able to come boldly forward with his (returning to Jung's wording), "'It seems to me like this.' And stand for it!" Continuing Jung states, "It must be the best you can do. No cheating, no flippancy or routine; then the devil is after you. You must be honest about whether it is really the best you can do. If it is the best before God that you can do, then you can count on things going the right way. But it may be the wrong way. We go through difficult things; that is fate."⁴⁷ Notice the emphasis here. Immersed in the patient's material, it is the analyst that must do the best he can before God. He that must

---

⁴⁵ C. G. Jung, *C. G. Jung Speaking: Interviews and Encounters*, William McGuire and R. F. C. Hull, eds. (Princeton, N.J.: Princeton University Press, 1977), p. 360.

⁴⁶ *Ibid.* Although in this passage Jung refers to God and to "the unconscious" in substantializing terms, the reader will understand that what is important in our context is the dialectical character of the thinking which interpretation involves. If the analyst can interpret boldly, it is because he is open to his interpretation going under and across into a better, truer one.

⁴⁷ *Ibid.* Wisely, Jung immediately follows up his statement about things going the right way if one does one's best before God with the sentence, "But it may be the wrong way." With respect to the dialectic of negation that he intimates in these terms, compare the following passage from Emerson: "You are preparing with eagerness to go and render a service to which your talent and your taste invite you, the love of men and the hope of fame. Has it not occurred to you that you have no right to go, unless you are equally willing to be prevented from going?" Ralph W. Emerson, "The Over-Soul," in *Selected Essays*, Larzer Ziff, ed. (New York: Penguin Books, 1982), p. 222. Also compare the following statement from Jung: "If a man is contradicted by himself and [...] knows that he contradicts himself, he is individuated." Letter to H. A. Murray, August 1956, Jung, *Letters*, vol. 2, p. 324.

vicariusly put the soul situation into words. And here, drawing again upon Hegel, we may further note that the task of the analyst, like that of the philosopher, "is to submerge his freedom in [the content, the phenomenon at hand] and let it be moved by its own [the phenomenon's own] nature,"[48] this on the assumption that, as the philosopher and Hegel scholar Charles Taylor puts it, "If the argument follows a dialectical movement, then this must be in the things themselves, not just in the way we reason about them."[49] Of course, it must immediately be added that this is what reason is, what insight, interiority, and truth are—the sublation of the difference between subject and object, self and other, knower and known, i.e., I in the speculative sense. And it is this—this "'I' that is a 'We' and 'We' that is an 'I',"[50] to again return to that expression of Hegel's—that the analyst, when speaking in the first person vicarius, attempts to let speak through him.

So much, then, for Jung's encouragement with respect to the making of speculative interpretations. Turning to Giegerich I am immediately reminded of his similarly "flesh of my flesh" or "mind of my mind" interpretation-emboldening statement, "psychology begins where any phenomenon (whether physical or mental, 'real' or fantasy image) is interiorized absolute-negatively into itself, and I find myself in its internal infinity. This is what it takes; psychology cannot be had for less."[51] Succinctly descriptive of the speculative turn in analytical psychology, this is an important passage. And when cited in our context three of its words are of especial importance—its author's bold declaration that "I find myself" in the matter at hand. Restating the maxim with the emphasis placed upon these words it may readily be added that on each interpretive occasion the kind of insight that is deserving of the name "psychology," produces itself, freshly and anew, via the analyst's or psychologist's giving voice to the phenomenon he is concerned with (in the context of psychotherapy,

---

[48] Cited by Charles Taylor, *Hegel* (Cambridge: Cambridge University Press, 1975), p. 129. The sentence referred to by Taylor is from section 58 of Hegel's *Phenomenology of Spirit,* not section 48 as he indicates.

[49] *Ibid.*

[50] Hegel, *PhS,* § 177, p. 110.

[51] Giegerich, "Is the Soul 'Deep'?—Entering and Following the Logical Movement of Heraclitus' 'Fragment 45'," in *CEP* IV, pp. 161-162.

to the patient's material) *as I*—which is also to say, as or in the register of what we have been calling "the first person vicarius." For the I that is referred to here is not the empirical subject, existing beforehand, but in the spirit of what Jung called "the coming to consciousness of the psychic process itself," the speculative subject that only gives rise to itself as the result of the phenomenon at hand obtaining self-character through its being interiorized into itself.

Ordinarily, of course, the phenomenon that a science is concerned with, whatever that may be, is conceived of as being the object of consciousness, the other of the observing subject. Subject and object, knower and objectivity negative to knowing, are kept neatly apart via the conventionally drawn difference of consciousness. "But for psychology," as Giegerich writes in a related passage, "there is no Other. Or the other that there is is 'the soul's own other,' its internal other, itself *as* other. 'The soul' is self-relation."[52] Expressed less concisely, the insight to be fathomed here is that what may variously be referred to as "psychology," "the soul," and the "I" has concept-character, not in the sense of some already conceived concept applied from without, but via the actuosity of the relation that relates itself to itself in the matter at hand. And here I should add that it is as the upshot of this that substance becomes known in essential regards, not only as an object of consciousness, but as subject, too.

But what does it mean, "relating itself to itself in the matter at hand"? In yet another key passage, Giegerich brings clarity to this question by likening whatever the phenomenon may be that psychology studies to a mirror in which the soul is reflected. "The psychological question," he writes, "is not, cannot be, what and how the soul *is*, but how the soul is *reflected* in its manifestations. [...] psychology is the study of the *reflection* in some mirror and not the study of *what* the mirror is the reflection *of*."[53] We can readily understand the distinction that Giegerich draws here by considering for a moment how it is exemplified in Jung's writings. When addressing himself to such topics as alchemy, flying saucers, the Trinity and the Mass, Jung was in each case not interested in the externals that these purportedly reflect. He was not in his studies of

---

[52] Giegerich, et. al., *Dialectics and Analytical Psychology: The El Capitan Canyon Seminar* (New Orleans: Spring Journal Books, 2005), p. 26.

[53] Giegerich, *CEP* vol. VI, p. 131-132.

medieval alchemy interested in literal gold-making or in how through its laboratory work with material substances it became a forerunner of modern chemistry. Nor in the case of UFO reports and religious ideas was he interested in the question of whether flying saucers actually exist or in questions concerning the existence or non-existence of God. For psychology's interest, whatever the phenomenon may be—a cultural document or historical event, a dream or a symptom—has rather to do with discerning what the phenomenon of its interest's appearing as it has reflects with respect to consciousness, mindedness, "the soul." And this, of course (though perhaps not so obviously), is the analyst's concern as well: to discern, not merely what the patient's material would seem to immediately reflect about him in his positivity as the person he is, but how the soul is exhibited, reflected, and made manifest in this material as the produced subject of a self-relation that, having been absolved from the difference of consciousness, exerts itself as truth, speaks up for itself as I.

Just as there is a kind of analysis that tries to account for why a person says what he says by reducing this to certain facts of his background, so there is another kind that wants to know, not why the patient is saying this, that, or the other thing, but *what* his statements and experiences mean in their substance and their truth, i.e., what the patient, when soulfully recognized, means at a soul level. What Giegerich had to say about psychology in the line from him we last quoted can thus be said about the I as well. The I, too, is a reflection in some mirror, and not the reflection of what the mirror is the reflection of. And this is so even though when I say "I", I am meaning "me". For although this is certainly the case, as the return from the otherness of all that I as me am not, my true I is irreducible and infinitely negative, which is why, when coming forward as I we put our "two-cents' worth" in, it is at once both a modest and a mighty sum.

Imitative I-statements, their difference from speculative ones

In an earlier section of this essay I briefly explored some of the objections that might reasonably be raised with respect to the analyst's saying I on behalf of the patient, and in that section I also attempted, in the spirit of saving the phenomenon, to differentiate such a manner of speaking from simply being put down to a kind of solidarity-imparting empathy with the patient and his plight. In this section I want to further elaborate upon this difference by contrasting what in the psychotherapy literature are called "imitative statements" with the kind of statement that is of concern to us here in which the analyst speaks for the patient in the first-person vicarius.

In his book, *Making Contact: Uses of Language in Psychotherapy*, Leston Havens discusses how a therapist, drawing upon the feelings and impressions evoked in him by a patient, may venture to speak out on the patient's behalf. When with a doubtful person, for example, he may simply offer up the statement, "How can I decide?", with a depressed one, "What hope is there?", and when with a fearful one, "Where does one find courage."[54] The merit of this style of expression is readily appreciated when we stop to consider the extent to which empathic statements can tend to "force patients to feel what the therapist believes they feel or should feel."[55] Especially in our day, when psycho-educational counselling has so much replaced the interpretive effort to work things out from scratch, is it likely that a well-meaning therapist may have his thumb on the scale in this way. In view of this a more neutral kind of empathy may be called for, one which "does not challenge, impress, or reach into what is private and defended," but rather, "increases or secures the other's self-possession," via the therapist's offering himself to the patient for the patient's purpose. Associated by Havens with the "doubling" that is practiced in psychodrama and in work with children, a further merit of such imitative statements lies in the alternative they provide to the therapist's asking questions too frequently. When questions are repeatedly addressed to them, patients may feel put on the spot, their therapy like an interrogation session.[56] What a relief, then, when the movement from consciousness to self-consciousness is instead mediated by means

---

[54] Havens, *Making Contact*, p. 27.

[55] *Ibid.*, p. 29.

[56] "The most tactful question in the world," writes Havens, "is still inquisitive and requests an answer. To some measure, it carries the memories of all questions that could not be answered or were shaming or damning to acknowledge." *Making Contact*, p. 107.

of comments and offerings of the imitative kind. All this, I believe, is evident in Havens's further examples. On behalf of a woman who, while confident in her beauty and desirous of getting married, was puzzled by a man who was highly inconsistent in the attention he showed her, Havens exclaimed at various points in the session, "Can he love me?" "Can I love Him?" "Why is he so elusive?" "*Aren't* I beautiful?" After capturing her interest with these statements, he then in closing returned to his position in the dyad saying, "I just hope he's worth your while."[57] In another case, this time with a male patient whose difficulties stemmed from his being in relation to others "either up front and naked or hidden away,"[58] Havens again found imitative statements to be helpful. "When I want something, it runs away," he was able to say for the patient with respect to one situation they had been discussing. "I have no rights," he said in another.[59]

This brief account of imitative statements is pretty much sufficient for our purposes here. It only needs to be added that while I hold such statements in high esteem and make frequent use of them in my work, their main importance in the present context is as a foil against which to throw into relief what is different about vicarius I-statements. We already know that vicarius I-statements have phenomenon character and are not, the way imitative ones are, a matter of technique. And to this it may be added that while in both kinds of statement the analyst speaks on behalf of the patient, the imitative and the vicarius ways of his doing so differ in that while the former mediates for the patient the taking up of a definite position, which of course is very important, the latter has rather to

---

[57] *Ibid.*, p. 32.

[58] *Ibid.*, p.37.

[59] It might be wondered if, when using imitative statements, the wires sometimes get crossed. Havens closes his chapter on imitative statements with an example in which this is the case. To a patient feeling badly that the treatment was taking so long, Havens said very earnestly, "I am responsible." Though Havens was here talking as himself, the patient at first took it as an imitative statement, something Havens was saying as him, for him, with respect to how he felt. But when it become apparent that this was not the case, and that Havens was indeed taking the responsibility, this was also helpful. As Haven puts it, "Only gradually did it become apparent that the *I* was really *me*, that the treatment was *my* responsibility, and that at least here, in this space, he might be given something of his own." Havens, *Making Contact*, p. 39.

do with presenting such a position, not in terms of the difference of consciousness as which the ego exists, but from the viewpoint of the soul, or as this might also be expressed, in the light of the psychological difference. This is not to say that the psychological difference is not already opened up to at least a minimal extent in the case of imitative statements. Even with them the soul side of the psychological difference weighs in, if only very lightly, via the analyst's speaking in the manner of the aforementioned "'I' that is a 'We' and … 'We' that is an 'I'." Thus, in formal regards, if not yet concretely, the rapport of the "we" into which the patient is drawn is as much at odds with and negating of his stick-in-the-mud self-identicalness (even when content-wise it may seem to merely reiterate, mirror or redouble this) as it is with respect to the ordinarily prevailing subject-over-against-object, self-over-against-other difference of consciousness. But as I just said, all this is only a very minimal expression of the form of subject and the viewpoint of the soul. It is not yet wholeheartedly enough the voice of the objective soul situation to fully warrant the epithet "vicarius."

The traditional meaning of vicarius and the analyst as *vicarius animæ*

At this juncture I want briefly to touch upon the history of the word that I have been using to indicate the subject of this essay. An old Latin term, "vicarius" means "substitute," "agent," "deputy." In Roman Catholicism it is used to indicate priests serving in one of the various ecclesiastical offices and of Popes in their role as Vicars of Christ. In the Anglican Church the term is used for the clergy more generally, even the most undistinguished parish priest being called a vicar. In these institutional contexts, the idea is of a cleric who mediates for the people their highest values and principles by modeling for them the example of Christ. In olden days, by acting in this way the priest looked after the relationship with God, much as the cobbler looked after everyone's shoes. Sacred matters were his specialty. Individuals and peoples did not have to establish this themselves.

Of course, we analysts are also mediators. As a matter of routine, we are all the time mediating between the patient and his inner, on the one hand, and between the patient and other people, on the other.

This very ordinary kind of mediation, however, is too horizontally oriented to warrant the term vicarius as its identifier. I say "horizontal" here because, for all their difference from each other, that which is intrapsychic (e.g., inner images, feelings, emotions) and that which is interpersonal (i.e., people and their social dynamics) are alike in existing positively as things that can be pointed at on the horizontal plane of the ordinary difference of consciousness. The vicarius mediation that an analyst may additionally have to provide, by contrast, has a vertical character, as was formerly the case with priestly mediators. Perpendicular to people and the psychology they have, it has to do with discerning, representing, and subjectively giving voice to or speaking in the name, not of God any more or some religious matter, but of the logically negative successor of these, the logic or concept that invisibly and over our heads, so to speak, we live in and exist as in our times. And here, further to this point, we may again recall Jung's teaching that it is not so much that the psyche is in us, but rather we that are in the psyche.[60]

Now it is crucial to emphasize that the logic just spoken of, which can also be referred to as "the soul of the real," has gone through enormous form changes in the course of its history, as has the office of mediator in keeping with these. Whereas formerly, in those times when religion dominated, the soul had had the form of God, its mediator the form of priest, in our day, *post mortem Dei*, soul has the form of psychological phenomena, the mediator of these the form of analyst. Which is why, as we shall see in the next section, Giegerich has characterized the analyst as serving in the capacity of "*vicarius animae*" at times. But before we turn to his discussion of this, let us expand a little more upon the form change just mentioned.

Indicative of the movement from consciousness to self-consciousness, the positivity of religion's substantiated form of thought has given way during the last several centuries to the negativity of this come home to itself as the modern subject. Sweepingly illustrative of this movement is the contrast between, on the one hand, the God in the Old Testament story who, upon appearing to Moses as a bush that burned and yet was not consumed, identified himself as "I am that I am,"[61] and, on the other hand, the *cogito* of Descartes, the I-think of

---

[60] See note 15 on p. 6 above.
[61] *Exodus* 3:13.

Kant, and the statements about the I that have been cited above from Hegel, to name only these later philosophical thinkers. And Jung, too, took notice of this form change in formulating what he called his "psychology 'with soul'."⁶² Indeed, by his lights, modern psychology in general is to be conceived of as having arisen negatively, if I may put it this way, as the precipitate remainder of the religion that preceded it. "All ages before us," he declared, "believed in gods in some form or other. Only an unparalleled impoverishment of symbolism could enable us to rediscover the gods as psychic factors, that is, as archetypes of the unconscious."⁶³

Although Jung speaks here of "rediscover[ing] the gods," it is really a matter of a change from the soul having the form of gods to it having the form of subjectivity. Earlier I cited Jung as saying that psychology is not an explanation of the psychic process, but an expression of the coming to consciousness of this. Returning to this point in the present context, it is important to realize that despite what I just said concerning its provenance, psychology is not the *explanation* of the religion that proceeded it (though Freud, of course, regarded it as such). Having arisen in the wake of that earlier form of the soul, it is rather to be regarded as the *phenomenological expression* and *speculative result* of the soul's having obtained the form of subject. Expressing this in Hegelian terms we could say that the verticality of the relationship that had formerly been conceived in pictorial terms as God above and Man below has in the modern situation gone under and across to become the infinitely negative I,⁶⁴ and this,

---

⁶² Jung, *CW* 8 § 661, "[…] we can perhaps summon up courage to consider the possibility of a 'psychology *with* soul,' that is a psychology [*Seelenlehre*] based on the hypothesis of an autonomous mind [*Geist*]" (translation modified).

⁶³ Jung, *CW* 9i, § 50. With respect to this account of psychology's provenance the following statement of Jung's is also pertinent: "Whenever there exists some external form, be it an ideal or a ritual, by which all the yearnings and hopes of the soul are adequately expressed—as for instance in a living religion—then we may say the psyche is outside and there is no psychic problem, just as there is then no unconscious in our sense of the word. In consonance with this truth, the discovery of psychology falls entirely within the last decades, although long before that man was introspective and intelligent enough to recognize the facts that are the subject-matter of psychology." *CW* 10 § 159.

⁶⁴ The infinitely negative I is the I that is no longer merely the self-identical me, but rather, is just as much constituted by or as the return from the otherness of all

moreover, in a manner that preserves the verticality of the former relation, which is also to say, the gradient of that former difference, if only by being what may variously be described as the seriousness, rectitude, universality and integrity that I as me am capable of when, cognizant of what is and mindful of others, I am up to the situation in which I find myself, true to myself therein.[65]

But here it may be objected, is this not asking too much? It is no small feat to be up to the situations we find ourselves in, let alone to be a man in the place where no men are, as a saying from the Talmud admonishes.[66] Not even for those who have gone in for meditation, mindfulness, and techniques of the like. For they, too, may find, despite the mastery they have achieved with respect to regulating their thoughts and emotions, that they are just as daunted as anyone else when it comes to that "larger part of the soul that is outside the body."[67] A go-between may therefore be needed if there is to be any coming to terms with what Jung, updating this line from the alchemists, called the objective psyche. A mediator between the personalistic subjectivity of the individual and the objective subjectivity of the soul. Which is why Giegerich in one of his essays coins the term *"vicarius animae"* to designate the role of the psychotherapist.

Presenting problems in the light of the psychological difference

Giegerich's introduction of the term *vicarius animae* into our discourse has as its context a discussion of what the stance of the analytic therapist must be with respect to symptomatic suffering and presenting complaints. The therapist, he insists, must have

---

that I am not. Against the foil of all that I am not, I am thrown into relief on the soul side of the psychological difference as (infinitely negative) I.

[65] It may be added here, by way of an aside, that reflective of the verticality that is imparted by our being true to ourselves and our situation is the fitness of the names that we assign to the things of our lives and world. This aspect of our topic will be discussed in Part Three of this essay.

[66] "[…] in a place where there are no men, strive to be a man." Ben Zion Bokser, trans., *The Talmud: A Selection* (Mahwah, New Jersey: Paulist Press, 1989), p. 222.

[67] "maior autem animae [pars] extra corpus est." Sendivogius, "De Sulphere," *Musaeum Hermeticum* (1678). Cited by Jung in his 12 July, 1951 letter to Karl Kerényi, Jung, *Letters*, vol. 2, p. 19. See also: Jung, *CW* 12 § 396, 399.

acquired, both for himself and for his patient's sake, a steadfastness in the face of disturbing psychic material and distressing symptoms. He cannot, as would those who indulge in the prissy spirituality of what Goethe, Hegel, and others of their period critiqued under the heading of "the beautiful soul," eschew the horrible and the bizarre, the sick and the wrong, declaring these to be inhuman or unsoulful. On the contrary, and in keeping with our earlier reference to Jung's having taken up the *nil humanum a me alienum* adage as his duty, he must endeavor "to become the unshaken, unperturbed holding vessel for the patient's pathology."[68]

> My patient is entitled to expect from me a genuine composure vis-à-vis the horrid aspects of his story. *Gelassenheit*. I must be able to honestly *allow* his story *to be* the way it is, without wishing it to be otherwise. We might even say that I must, in some way, embrace it, to harbour it within myself. Despite its possibly horrid and inhuman appearance, and this means despite the fact that for me as empirical I (the human-all-too-human person or ordinary citizen) that I am, it may indeed be deeply upsetting or even frightening—nevertheless as therapist, as 'the *vicarius animae* on earth' (the representative of the soul standpoint in real life) I must accept it as *not*-alien and thus, with methodological awareness, give it its own place within the sphere of what is *humanum* and soulful. Each new pathology is a challenge and an invitation to me to conquer for myself the soul standpoint once again by overcoming myself as the "ego," the habitual everyday or man-on-the-street point of view, and so also my fear of or disgust for the abnormal.[69]

It will be noticed that the unflinching steadfastness that is central to Giegerich's characterization of the therapist as "the *vicarius animae* on earth" is conceived by him in terms of the psychological difference. Presented in this passage as the difference between the everyday viewpoint of the ego, on the one hand, and the analyst-mediated viewpoint of the soul, on the other, the psychological difference may also be figured as the difference between the horizontal and the vertical, as was discussed in the previous section. It must immediately be added, however, that ego and soul, horizontal

---

[68] Giegerich, *CEP* IV, p.503.
[69] *Ibid.*, pp, 503-504.

and vertical, are not in our day the symbolically hypostasized, already distinct substantial opposites that they were for our religious forebears. They are not for us, that is to say, two already existing entities or domains that we subsequently bring together. In modern times, it is rather a matter of our starting from the everyday level of the ego, from the horizontal and earthly, and producing the verticality of the soul's view of things via an act of interpretive insight and seeing-through. Just as in Homer's *The Odyssey* Menelaus holds the shapeshifting Proteus in an all-encompassing grip until a prophecy is wrung from him, and just as the alchemists placed the substances they were endeavouring to transform in a hermetically-sealed vessel, so it is that via the therapist's steadfastness in the face of the patient's material, no matter how distressing and disturbing that material may be, that the psychological difference is opened up and the standpoint of the soul achieved.

It is a matter of feeling, or as Giegerich further points out, of the therapist's access to and use of a special kind of feeling which is not emotional, in the sense of having feelings, but rational, in the sense of exercising judgment.[70] Identified by Jung as "the feeling function,"[71] it is the therapist's capacity to discern what is truly of psychological significance from what is not by means of this rational kind of feeling that is important in our context. And on this point, Giegerich could not be more adamant. "Without feeling," he writes, "the soul cannot be apperceived. Feeling in this [rational] sense is what has the power to connect modern consciousness with the soul-in-the-real across the gap of our fundamental alienation from it. The capacity to feel is the bridge across the psychological difference, the bridge also across and beyond our subjective positive or negative feelings, so that we may become open to the heart of what *is*."[72]

But what has the feeling described got to do with that more objective level of subjectivity which (like some voice crying in the wilderness) the analyst hears in the patient's situation even as at the

---

[70] Of course, by "exercising judgment," I do not mean "being judgmental" in the pejorative sense of that phrase. It is rather a matter of assessing whether, by its own standards, a particular phenomenon is in accord with its concept (this friend a true friend, for example).

[71] Jung, *CW* 6 § 723-729.

[72] Giegerich, *CEP* IV, p. 510.

same time he enunciates it on his behalf?[73] In a statement subsequent to those I have already cited, Giegerich explicitly connects this mediating, psychological difference-establishing proclivity of the feeling function with the vicariusly-mediated, more-than-egoic I. Feeling, he writes, "is that mode *in* the empirical I in which the I with its initial egoic survival interests has gone under, has learned to be silent—has *died* as 'the ego.' Feeling is the soul's ambassador, ally, advocate, 'fifth column' in the empirical person, ... the *vicarius animae*. And as such it is the *copula*, the *ligamentum* or *vinculum* in the sense of alchemy, between empirical man ('I') and the soul ... as well as between positive-factual reality and the Mercurial spirit 'imprisoned' in that reality."[74] So much, then, for the mediation that the analyst as *vicarius animae* provides. It only remains to be discussed how presenting problems, distressing symptoms, and the like can be insightfully grasped in their verticality and truth.

Giegerich has usefully observed that "What first appears as a content *of* consciousness is in truth the seed of what wants to become a radically new *form* of consciousness at large."[75] Adapting this adage to the terms of our present discussion, we could also say that what is at first apperceived *horizontally* via the ordinarily prevailing subject here/object there difference of consciousness is the pivot point of what wants to be known *vertically*, speculatively, overarchingly and conceptually as the sublation of that flat external difference. Only think in this connection of those by no means uncommon dreams in which the figure of the dreamer desperately tries to evade what seems to be an imminent calamity, the threat, for example, posed by a menacing pursuer. Usually, it takes the steadfastness of the analyst in the face of such fraught situations to

---

[73] I speak of the objective subjectivity of the patient's situation being heard by the analyst *even as and at the same time* he enunciates it. The italicized words indicate that it is not a matter of the analyst's first hearing and then articulating what is heard. Between the analyst's hearing and speaking there is rather a dialectical relation. The analyst dares to speak, i.e., to think out-loud (at times, to be sure, only inwardly and to himself), in order to hear what is to be heard in the first place. There is nothing to hear until he speaks. This is what it means to have left the ordinary prevailing subject here/object there difference of consciousness behind, or better said, to have sublated this ordinary difference.

[74] Giegerich, *CEP* IV, p. 511.

[75] *Ibid.*, p. 149. Cf., Giegerich, *The Soul's Logical Life*, pp. 147-148.

mediate for the dreamer the realization that the seemingly external other that the dream-I is intent on escaping *is its own other* and that what is happening on the ground, so to speak, has rather and more vertically to do with a transformation of consciousness, a changing of the mind. Beset by doubts, vexed by troubling anomalies, prey to second thoughts, the concept that the dreamer exists as (a.k.a. "the soul") is going through a self-negation. It is having to realize, as Giegerich puts it, "that the matter has all along *not* been what it had seemed to be," [76] which, at the same time, is already its being exposed to the new form of the matter, the new apperception of its objective situation, the new form of truth.

So there we have it. The point is made. In the psychotherapeutic context the epithet "vicarius" is only fitting for the mediation of what is vertical. It only remains to be added that in its first immediacy the vertical corresponds, on the one hand, to the steadfastness of the analyst in the face of negations, and on the other, to those phenomena that are implicitly vertical in that they stick out like a sore thumb from the horizontal dimension, or as a stumbling block along the path of the ordinarily prevailing difference of consciousness. Hearing of such phenomena as he listens to the patient's account of his presenting problem, the analyst feels their surplus value, the import for the mind of what is suffered in the flesh, and "interpret[ing] from above downwards,"[77] as Jung once put it, speaks accordingly. And so it is—as the comeuppance of a truth hurts dialectic—that the verticality of the soul is produced, the soul side of the psychological difference insighted.[78] Changed-

---

[76] Giegerich, *CEP* IV, p. 472.

[77] Jung, *CW* 14 § 205.

[78] Pertinent to the seeing through of suffering that is experienced on an ego level to the suffering on the logical level that consciousness in the larger sense experiences in the course of its dialectical unfolding is a passage from the Christian Apocrypha's *Acts of John* in which Jesus declares: "You hear that I suffered, yet I suffered not; and that I suffered not, yet I did suffer; and that I was pierced, yet I was not wounded; that I was hanged, yet I was not hanged; that blood flowed from me, yet it did not flow, and, in a word, that what they say of me, I did not endure, but what they do not say, those things I did suffer. Now what these are, I secretly show you .... You must know me, then, as the torment of the logos, the piercing of the logos, the blood of the logos, the wounding of the logos, the fastening of the logos." Willis Barnstone, ed., *The Other Bible* (New York: Harper & Row, 1984), p. 420.

up by what it wants to but is unable to keep at bay, consciousness becomes self-consciousness. And this it achieves, in no small part, due to the analyst's vicariusly bringing forth from the patient's situation some version of that question, so productive of speculative insight, that Jung had raised on his dreamer's behalf, "Who am I that all this should happen to me?"

Part Two

SPECULATIVE INTERPRETATION AND THE POETICS OF THE I

Cultivating the requisite facility

In Part One of this essay, the phenomenal character of what I there called vicarius I-statements was discursively highlighted. Wholly different from occasions when analysts speak to their patients in accordance with the ordinarily prevailing difference of consciousness and as if from some theoretical vantage point outside, vicarius I-statements have to do with what Jung called "the coming to consciousness of the psychic process itself," which is also to say, with the symptoms and situations that the patients are troubled by obtaining by means of such statements the form of the subject, the form of the cure. Fathomed in this light, therapy has to do with the sublating of an "already, but not yet" dialectic. Equivocating as a subject, lagging behind his constitution as an I, the patient tends to construe those meetups with himself he calls his experiences in external terms, unaware of the extent to which his wider consciousness and larger personality are out-pictured in the events that befall him, the world he apperceives and imparts himself to. The analyst, by contrast, hears what the patient tells him as being indicative, not only of the patient, but of the patient and his world, and speaks up for him on that basis. Under his breath, he raises on behalf of the patient the question—"to be or not to be," or as this might be adapted, "to self or not to self?"—and then, making bold, vicariusly intones a soliloquy of the I, saying the truth of the situation as best he can. And here again it is important to emphasize that such statements are not a matter of doling out knowledge in the manner of an educator, or platitudes in the manner of a wise teacher or priest, but of giving voice to the subjectivity of the situation in such a way that all that the patient has falteringly taken stock of in what may metaphorically be described as a "counting on his fingers" mode is brought into the oneness of the concept, the oneness of the I, by its now, as it were, being "counted in the head."

But the question arises. How is the sensibility conducive to providing such statements to be cultivated in the analyst? We already know that in order to be authentic the I must give rise to itself via the mediation of the material at hand, and not be based upon some theory that is brought to bear upon the psychic process from outside. The analyst, as Jung put it, must not know beforehand,[1] but must rather immerse himself in the soul-situation presented by the patient and then, by thinking the unity of the unity and difference of its various aspects and moments, produce the subject, self, or I as the speculative result of this process. Now my reference here is to the I as "speculative result" because this subject is born out of the interpretative process. It comes, if it comes at all, in the way poetic insights come. Creativity and inspiration are involved. It is like what the poet Emily Dickinson was getting at with her characterization of art as "a house that tries to be haunted."[2] Psychotherapy, too, is an art in this sense. It, too, a house that tries to be haunted, in its case by the soul, soul in its modern shape as speculative I.

It might be wondered then, given what has just been said, how analysts and psychotherapists are to be trained. In this connection, though without reference to our specific topic, Giegerich has usefully advised that the training of analysts and analytic psychotherapists should be largely a matter of cultivating and exercising the mind to make the complex dialectical movements that are required if a truly psychological understanding of the situations and case material they will face in the consulting room is to be attained.[3] Something very much like this, I believe, holds true with respect to the cultivation of the sensibility conducive to the vicarius articulation of the soul as I. The analyst's ability, or better, susceptibility, to speaking in the first person vicarius is dependent upon his or her being able to draw from

---

[1] Jung, *CW* 16 § 197; 9i § 528.
[2] Emily Dickinson, *The Letters of Emily Dickinson*, 3 vols., ed., T. Johnson and T. Ward (Cambridge: Belknap Press of Harvard University Press, 1958), L459a.
[3] Giegerich, *The Soul's Logical Life,* p. 277.

the material at hand the categories by which it is to be interpreted, while giving to this at the same time the form of subject. In this second part of the essay, my aim is to contribute to this susceptibility, and to the cultivation of its resident facility, by means of a series of shorter and longer discussions of a diverse range of inspiring texts, edifying expositions, poetic insights, and dialectical reflections drawn from notes set down over many years that I regard as being pertinent to the training of the mind of the practitioner for his or her mediating role as *vicarius animae*.

The visionary character of the soul as I

Mindful of Jung's advisement that "only the smallest part of the psyche [...] presents itself in the medical consulting room,"[4] I begin this series of reflections far away from what I ultimately want to get close to, which is of course those exchanges between the therapist and the patient in which the therapist says I on the patient's behalf.[5]

In response to the question, "What is soul?", Aristotle in his *De Anima* avers that soul is to things what sight is to the eye. Take sight from the eye, he further observes, and an eye is an eye no more, but merely a mass of tissues, an orb of flesh.[6] When thinking over what was discussed in Part One of this essay concerning the analyst as *vicarius animae*, and now, further to this, of the training of the mind that is necessary for him or her to serve in this capacity, I find that this analogy of Aristotle's (or rather, glossing differences, a retrospectively changed up sense of this analogy![7]) readily joins up in

---

[4] Jung, *Letters* 2, p. 307. 17 June 1956, to Nelson.

[5] This beginning, as I just put it, "far away from what I ultimately want to get close to," is conceived in the light of the paradox that a truly *psychological* psychology has to start in the soul in order to get to the soul. For more on this topic see Giegerich, *The Soul's Logical Life*, p. 21.

[6] Aristotle, *De Anima*, Book II, chapter 1.

[7] Although in the present context my citing of Aristotle is mediated from the outset by what I also will be quoting from Jung and Hegel, I should at least pay for the licence I am affording myself in this regard by noting that in its own context Aristotle's statement, "[...] if the eye were an animal, sight would be its soul," is used by him to indicate soul as the "essential whatness" of a matter of interest. In another analogy, Aristotle offers that if an axe were a living creature its body would be the iron and wood of which it is made, whereas its soul would

my mind with that oft-quoted passage from the *Visions Seminars* in which Jung declares that "[...] behind the impressions of the daily life—behind the scenes—another picture looms up, covered by a thin veil of facts,"[8] and I am inspired as it does so to characterize the I that we have been concerned with in these pages as the sight—the soul—of persons and worlds, even as, insightfully imparting itself in the form of names, this I that I am, and that we as a people are, gives voice in the same breath to the thought as which, "bone of my bone, flesh of my flesh," the object side or Eve side of the ordinarily prevailing difference of consciousness, which is also to say, the world that we are ever again the word-finding, name-giving Adams of, exists and obtains its perfection. As for the second part of Aristotle's statement, the part about an eye not being an eye at all if deprived of the sight that is its soul, the parallel to this that may be drawn here is that without the I, that is, without that self-determining, insight-producing, reflexive first-person pronoun, Man, too, as Yeats so aptly put it, is but "a paltry thing,/A tattered coat upon a stick."[9] And it is the same again the other way around, for what is the world without the subject that beholds it?

---

be that which made it an axe, in other words, its capacity to chop. It will be noticed that in the case of this second analogy the soul or "essential whatness" of the axe is not seen by the sight of the literal eye, but by that of the knowing mind, even as the mind's own essential whatness is disclosed via its knowing and naming the soul of such a thing. In keeping with this, it should also be noted that it is the same for the sight that is the soul of the eye. The eye does not see itself. Rather, *that* seeing that sees that sight is the eye's soul is an insight known by the mind, which is also to say, it is something that I know.

[8] C. G. Jung, *The Visions Seminars*, Book One (Zürich: Spring Publications, 1976), p. 8. In terms of its original context, Jung's statement that "another picture looms up" has to do with the interpreter making a hermeneutic shift from thing-like psychic image (in the dream he discusses, the image of a doctor who lives by the sea) to the psychologically apperceived *concept* that such an image discloses to the thinking mind (in Jung's example, the archetypal concept of the true doctor, soul doctor, or medicine man). In addition to this, I like to supplement Jung's meaning with another by comparing the cited statement with a text in which he speaks of the ego's being taught by its limits that it is not identical with the self, and this, moreover (and here is the other sense of "another picture loom[ing] up"), in such a way that "in *this self we appear wondrously strange to ourselves.*" For the full quotation, see page 19, footnote 39 in Part One above.

[9] W. B. Yeats, "Sailing to Byzantium," *W. B. Yeats Selected Poetry*, A. Norman Jeffares, ed. (London: Pan Books, 1974), p. 104.

In his memoirs, Jung highlights this, let us call it, cosmogonic significance of the I and its provenance, with a story he tells of having, while on safari in East Africa, departed from his companions so as to gaze over the gigantic herds of animals moving across the savanna below where he stood, savoring as he did so the feeling of being utterly alone. As he watched the vast herds moving below him like slow rivers, he was amazed by the silent atmosphere of the scene. "This was the stillness of the eternal beginning, the world as it had always been, in the state of non-being, for until then no one had been present to know that it was this world."[10] Why, it was quite as if, Jung continues, he was "the first human being to recognize that this was the world, but who did not [yet] know that in this moment he had first really created it."[11] Of course, the last part of that statement doesn't hold because, differently from earlier humans as he here conceives of them, Jung did know. He knew that by going along with what this primeval setting evoked in him, he was arranging an experience for himself. But be that as it may, it was from this experience that "the cosmic meaning of consciousness became overwhelmingly clear" to him. And what was that meaning? With the sight of those magnificent animal herds still fresh in his mind's eye, and after citing the alchemical dictum, "What nature leaves imperfect, the art perfects," Jung declares, "Man, I, in an invisible act of creation put the stamp of perfection on the world by giving it objective existence."[12]

So, there we have it. Just as the soul of the eye is its capacity to see, so the soul of man resides in, or better, produces itself as, the

---

[10] Jung, *MDR,* p. 255.

[11] *Ibid.* In a personal communication (30 October 2020), W. Giegerich corrects the translation: "The Jung passage would even be more fitting if you had not had to rely on the wrong and nonsensical translation of *MDR.* Jung's text reads: "Da war ich nun der erste Mensch, der erkannte, daß dies die Welt war und sie durch sein Wissen in diesem Augenblick erst wirklich geschaffen hatte." Roughly translated: 'In this situation [or Thus] I was [in the sense of 'had become', 'had turned into'] the first man who cognized that this was the world and [who] had in this moment first truly created it through his knowing.' No 'as if' and the opposite of 'who did not [yet] know'. It is his *knowing* (the *event* or occurrence of consciousness, of knowing) that according to Jung completes the creation, i.e., that alone bestows true being to it. Either the *MDR* translators had a different text to be translated or they made a mess of the translation."

[12] Jung, *MDR,* p. 255.

logic-revealing, truth-disclosing, name-conferring reflection of what *is* into itself. Expanding upon this, it may further be said, that as the relation that relates itself to itself in the matter at hand, soul (man's soul) is the pivot point or inflection point wherein the unity of the unity and difference of all we are exposed to and aware of comes together, as it were, within the apperceptive unity of the I, much as letters come together in the making of words, words in the making of the statements that we say.[13] —Very different, this, from the subjectivity-dissociating empiricist mindset for which "objects perceived as objects are soon rendered fixed and dead."[14] For indeed, in contrast to this, Jung's "Man, I ..." not only gives the world its objective existence, but produces itself at the same time as a subjectivity that is absolved from the abstractly construed subject here/object there difference of consciousness, and this, moreover, in such a way that object, other, and world become conscious of themselves, known from within. And here now, further to these reflections, I am reminded of a passage from Hegel in which a logic very similar to that which is operative in what we have just heard from Jung is especially well expressed.

> When I look at something (*Im Anschauen*), what I look at is in me – for it is I, after all, who look at it; it is *my* looking. Spirit steps out of this looking, and looks at its looking – i.e., it looks at the object as its own, at the object [now] cancelled as a being [and taken as] image. In the looking, Spirit is the image. For it, insofar as it is consciousness, [the object] is a being that is severed from the I. For us, however, it is the unity of both [i.e., its independent being and the I]. It becomes clear to Spirit that it [i.e., Spirit itself] is in and for itself (*an und für sich*) – but to begin with, in the looking, Spirit is only in itself. It compliments this [being-in-itself] with the for-itself, with negativity, separation from the in-

---

[13] Here, in relation to this analogy to combining letters to make words and words to make meanings, I am reminded of a comment Giegerich makes further to his having defined psychological phenomena as "events of meaning": "'Events of meaning' means that psychic occurrences are in themselves linguistic (linguistic *as events*, i.e., even prior to and without being literally put into words"). *CEP* III, p. 175.

[14] Samuel Taylor Coleridge. Cited in M.H. Abrams*, et. al., The Norton Anthology of English Literature* (New York: W. W. Norton, 1975), p. 1588.

itself, and goes back into itself. It takes its first self as an object, i.e., the *image, Being* as *mine,* as negated (*als aufgehobnes*).[15]

The words in this passage that we should particularly take heed of are those having to do with spirit stepping out of its simple looking to look at its looking. Returning to Jung, it can readily be seen that this was the kind of looking that his African experience was about. Jung did not merely look at the animals moving below him in vast herds as so many empirical objects. He looked as his looking, or as he also put this, at "the miracle of reflecting consciousness."[16] And the upshot of this was that he, his subjectivity, or as he earlier referred to this, "Man, I," was recognized as "indispensable for the completion of creation." In Jung's words, man "is the second creator of the world, who alone has given to the world its objective existence—without which, unheard, unseen, silently eating, giving birth, dying, heads nodding through hundreds of millions of years, it would have gone on in the profoundest night of non-being down to its unknown end."[17]

Briefly reiterating what has been discussed thus far, let it simply be said that just as Aristotle characterized the soul as being to things what sight is to the eye,[18] so is what Jung with reference to his panoramic vision from the vista above the Athi Plains calls "Man, I" to the "great process of being." And this, moreover, is what Hegel was getting at when he famously said that "everything turns on grasping and expressing the True, not only as *Substance,* but equally as *Subject.*"[19]

---

[15] Hegel, *The Philosophy of Spirit* (Jena Lectures 1805-6) Part I. Spirit according to its Concept. www.marxists.org/reference/archive/hegel/works/jl/ch01a.htm, (accessed 23 October 2020).

[16] Jung, *MDR*, p. 339.

[17] *Ibid.*, p. 256.

[18] As previously noted, soul, for Aristotle, is the "essential whatness" of a thing, his examples of this being sight in the case of the eye and the capacity to chop in the case of an axe. In keeping with this, man's soul resides in his capacity to be conscious of what is, or more acutely, to be conscious of being conscious of what is.

[19] Hegel, *PhS*, § 17, p. 10.

There is another resonance between Jung and Hegel that is pertinent to the training of our minds for vicarius service. In a passage that follows directly upon the earlier one we quoted in which Hegel speaks of our looking at our looking, the great philosopher brings us closer to the consulting room, if only by means of the very slender connection that whereas Jung looked out and down over the vast herds of animals migrating across the Athi Plains of Africa, Hegel, after having removed himself in a similar manner to the heights of speculative philosophical thought, surveys the dissembled array of images which move just as unconsciously and proto-subjectively in the inner of our human nature.

> This image [which is not just of something other, because it is indicative at the same time of our own seeing—G.M.] belongs to Spirit. Spirit is in possession of the image, is master of it. It [the image] is stored in the Spirit's treasury, in its Night. The image is unconscious, i.e., it is not displayed as an object for representation. The human being is this Night, this empty nothing which contains everything in its simplicity—a wealth of infinitely many representations, images, none of which occur to it directly, and none of which are not present. This [is] the Night, the interior of [human] nature, existing here – pure Self – [and] in phantasmagoric representations it is night everywhere: here a bloody head suddenly shoots up and there another white shape, only to disappear as suddenly. We see this Night when we look a human being in the eye, looking into a Night which turns terrifying. [For from his eyes] the night of the world hangs out toward us.[20]

It may not be obvious how human beings, the way Hegel describes them in this passage, correspond to the therapist and the patient in psychotherapy. The patient in front of us blinks in the daylight as he tells us what he sees and imagines, thinks, believes, and feels. When he looks at us there may be earnestness in his glance, or a smile in his eye, perhaps. A great richness of expressions is possible. So what then are we to make of Hegel's ghoulish description of the human being, and thus in a smaller sense of the

---

[20] Hegel, *The Philosophy of Spirit* (Jena Lectures 1805-6) Part I. Spirit according to its Concept. www.marxists.org/reference/archive/hegel/works/jl/ch01a.htm, (accessed 23 October 2020).

patient, too, as the negative register of all that there is, or he as puts this, as "the night of the world"?

We are used to the idea of an unconscious mind, and used, as well, to Freud and Jung having thought of this as being like some Africa within, primitive and primeval. As for Hegel's characterization of the human psyche as a night-like abyss that is emptily potentiated by a veritable infinity of images, "none of which occur to it directly, and none of which are not present," this is familiar to us in the notion of overdetermination. Like the shades in the underworld, the images of the psyche roil in the seething cauldron of their latency. "Shoot[ing] up [...] only to disappear as suddenly," they are comparable to the letters of a word jumble which thought creates itself as the reading of. Or, since as Jung insists, we must not fall for the seductive power of fantasy images,[21] the images at the same time are just as much like the shadows on the wall of Plato's cave that the philosopher, whom we may regard as the representative of the I that is of concern to us in this essay, must turn away from if he is to form a true conception of what is. And this, I would offer, is pretty much what Jung did when, turning away from his companions so as to relish the feeling of being "utterly alone," he arranged that experience for himself of being the first man. As was just discussed, after turning away from his companions his experience of himself as the culminating and consciousness-conferring element in creation was achieved by his capacity for this being actualized by its being thrown vertically into relief against the herds of animals which he could now describe as "unheard, unseen, silently eating, giving birth, dying, heads nodding through hundreds of millions of years, ... in the profoundest night of non-being down to its unknown end."[22] Can a similar claim be made with respect to the psychological I and the human traffic? Time and again, have the various historical junctures and rupture points that our species was challenged by during the course of its own higher

---

[21] Jung's statement, "the aim of individuation is nothing less that to divest the self of the false wrappings of the persona on the one hand, and the suggestive power of primordial images on the other," *CW* 7 § 269. Cf., *MDR*, pp. 186-187; *CW* 7 § 161; *CW* 4 § 410.

[22] Jung, *MDR*, p. 256.

development been the successive pivot points of a similarly consciousness-establishing and mere-being sublating reflective distancing? Or to ask this question again, this time with respect to the self-consciousness epitomizing psychological I, is this, too, the negation negating speculative result of our otherwise separate or abstract subjectivities being thrown into relief against "the night of the world hang[ing] out toward us" from each other eyes?

We have to realize that Hegel's vision here is as much an arrangement or fabrication as was Jung's. He already knew that the self-consciousness that is our distinction as human subjects is constituted by the return from the otherness of another self-consciousness.[23] He knew, if I may put it this way, that below the level of this attainment, achieved and successively changed up many times in the history of the logical life of the soul, that our seeing and being terrified by the night of the world hanging out toward us as we look into the abyss of the inwardly-focused eyes of another person is a matter of our seeing "the stick in our brother's eye and not the beam in our own" (Matthew 7: 3-5). For the look that we in our abstract self-identity cast upon our neighbour may, at first glance, be just as abysmal, just as terrifying. Or rather, it would be so except that in that twinkling of an eye in which glances are exchanged *we* reciprocally mediate for one another the negation of that consciousness that is separately and abstractly limited to merely knowing benightedly *as substance* what can also be known, in the light of this negation negating reciprocity of our looking at each other looking at each other, etc., *as subject*.

Just as truth, according to Hegel, is the unity of identity and difference,[24] so is the mutual recognition via which we establish the

---

[23] Hegel, *PhS*, § 167, p. 105, §184, p. 112.

[24] Hegel, "The claims of separation must be admitted just as much as those of identity. When identity and separation are placed in opposition to each other, both are absolute, and if one aims to maintain identity through the nullification of the dichotomy, then [identity and dichotomy] remain opposed to each other. Philosophy must give the separation into subject and object its due. By making both separation and the identity, which is opposed to it, equally absolute, however, philosophy has only posited separation conditionally, in the same way that such an identity – conditioned as it is by the nullification of its opposite – is also only relative. Hence, the Absolute itself is the identity of identity and non-identity;

reasons and shared meanings that are our truths the unity of the identity and difference of our seeming at "first glance" to see eye to eye, on the one hand, and the night of the world hanging out of our respective gazes producing uncertainty and "second thoughts," on the other. The other seeing us, confirming, and recognizing us, is also (inasmuch as what can only be seen by the mind is simultaneously involved) thinking us, disconfirming and negating our simple self-identicalness. And this is a two-way street. Our looking at his looking at our looking, *ad infinitum*, raises for us both the periscope of the mind's eye and mind's I, even as it mediates for us each the transition from consciousness to self-consciousness.

We see in the otherness of each other's eyes, "here a bloody head suddenly shoot[ing] up and there another white shape […] disappear[ing] as suddenly," as Hegel impressionistically conveying the negativity that each implicitly more conscious subject metes out for the other put it in the passage cited. What changes this up such that consciousness becomes self-consciousness is a function of the sustaining of the vis-à-vis described. It is what Hegel was getting in his famous text about "tarry[ing] with the negative":

> … the life of the spirit is not the life that shrinks from death and keeps itself untouched by devastation, but rather the life that endures it and maintains itself in it. It wins its truth only when, in utter dismemberment, it finds itself. It is this power, not as something positive, which closes its eyes to the negative as when we say of something that it is nothing or is false, and then having done with it, turn away and pass on to something else; on the contrary, spirit is this power only by looking the negative in the face, and tarrying with it. This tarrying with the negative is the magical power that converts it into being.[25]

Although analytic psychotherapy is conducted for the most part in an atmosphere of sympathetic support and solidarity, it is also rife with

---

being opposed and being one are both together in it." *The Difference between Fichte's and Schelling's System of Philosophy.* https://www.marxists.org/reference/ archive/ hegel/works/fs/ch03.htm (accessed 3 January 2023).

[25] Hegel, *PhS*, § 32, p. 19.

moments in which both parties must tarry with the negation that each in their differences from each other are such that, negating their negation of each other, what Jung called "Man, I" and Hegel called the "'I' that is a 'We' and [the] 'We' that is an 'I'"[26] may constitute itself within what we may now call the speculative dimension of the transference. Upon hearing the description of a life experience or dream, the analyst, while remaining firmly seated in his chair, departs, so to speak, from the subject here/object there mentality of the clinic to enter *à corps perdu* into the settings and landscapes of his patient's night. Like Jung gazing out at the rivers of animals below him on the Athi plain, the analyst exposes himself to the inscapes of his patient's, or better, of "the soul's" night such that the shapes and figures of this obtain within his overarching conceptual grasp the conceptual form of the self as I and a statement in the first person vicarius may be enunciated.

The poetic I as *vicarius animæ*

Jung's having vicariusly said his "Man, I" for us all while on safari in Africa, together with the passages from Aristotle and Hegel that I quoted in order to highlight the speculative character of such I-actuating self experience, becomes readily practicable in the context of psychotherapy through a consideration of those passages, so very frequent in poetry, in which a poet speaks in what I have been calling in these pages "the first person vicarius." No doubt, one of the greatest and most thoroughgoing examples of this is to be found in the poetry of Walt Whitman. Reading Whitman, the analytic psychotherapist will readily get a sense of how the valve in his own throat may be loosened such that he, too, can speak as the subject of the life situations and dream situations he is apprised of by his patients.[27] Now by subject here

---

[26] *Ibid.*, § 177, p. 110.

[27] It is only for the purpose of reflecting upon our topic of vicarius I-statements that we are citing in this section and the next from Whitman's poetry. Whitman's status as a poet, his place in the history of the logical life of the American soul, as well as questions that might reasonably be asked as to whether his poetry begins and ends in the mystic immediacy of a Beautiful Soul mentality or is actually more incisive and negation-born than that (its sensuous directness and seeming naivety

I mean pretty much what Hegel meant when he wrote of "an 'I' that is a 'We' and a 'We' that is an 'I',"[28] or, again, what Jung was getting at when he wrote that "the self comprises infinitely more than a mere ego [...] It is as much one's self, and all other selves, as the ego."[29] In Whitman's poetry the I by which the poet declares himself is an "I [that] contain[s] multitudes."[30] Vicariusly giving voice to the great diversity of the American soul in the same breath as he refers to himself in the first person, Whitman's I, which as he says is "not contained between my hat and boots,"[31] is the "return from the otherness" (as Hegel would say) of the great multitude of the people and situations, endeavours and occupations, events, happenings, and wonders, both natural and industrial, that he catalogues in the form of the vast number of one or two line "sight poems" of which his poetry is composed.

> The sharphoofed moose of the north, the cat on the housesill,
>   the chickadee, the prairie dog,
> The litter of the grunting sow as they tug at her teats,
> The brood of the turkeyhen, and she with her halfspread wings
> *I see in them and myself the same law.*[32]

Reading on we again and again find that the same speculative self-relation diversely reiterates itself throughout the entirety of his great poem, *Leaves of Grass:*

> The pure contralto sings in the organ loft,
> The carpenter dresses his plank .... the tongue of his foreplane
>   whistles its wild ascending lisp,

---

being indicative of what in PDI is called the restored position), is beyond the scope of the present discussion.

[28] Hegel, *PhS,* §177, p. 110.

[29] Jung, *CW* 8 § 432. In the next sentence, Jung writes, "Individuation does not shut one out from the world, but gathers the world to oneself."

[30] The full verse is especially felicitous in relation to psychology as the discipline of interiority: "Do I contradict myself?/ Very well then .... I contradict myself;/ I am large .... I contain multitudes." Whitman, *Leaves of Grass,* Malcolm Cowley, ed. (New York: Penguin Books, 1976), p. 85, lines 1314-1316.

[31] *Ibid.,* p. 31, line 124.

[32] *Ibid.,* p. 36, lines 241-245, italics, mine.

> The married and unmarried children ride home to their Thanksgiving dinner [...][33]

For several pages the poet extends the list of figures and scenes which he claims for his verse. And then, pausing only very briefly before going on to write about "The little one who sleeps in its cradle," the "suicide [who] sprawls on the bloody floor,"[34] the runaway slave he allows to shelter with him and all the rest, he intimates that "these one and all tend inward to me, and I tend outward to them,/ And as such as it is to be of these more or less I am."[35] Reading such statements we are immediately reminded of Jung's having written in the "The Psychology of the Transference," of our "meet[ing] ourselves time and again in a thousand disguises on the path of life."[36] And there is another passage in Jung's writings that is equally Whitmanesque. I refer to those lines in which the psychologist advises "Anyone who wants to know the human psyche [...] to put away his scholar's gown, bid farewell to his study, and wander with human heart through the world. [For] there, in the horrors of prisons, lunatic asylums and hospitals, in drab suburban pubs, in brothels and gambling-hells, in the salons of the elegant, the Stock Exchanges, Socialist meetings, churches, revivalist gatherings and ecstatic sects, through love and hate, through the experience of passion in every form in his own body, he would reap richer stores of knowledge than textbooks a foot thick could give him, and he will know how to doctor the sick with real knowledge of the human soul."[37]

But let us return (now from the otherness of Jung!) to what psychotherapy can learn from Whitman with respect to vicarius I-statements.

---

[33] *Ibid.*, p. 37, lines 257-259.

[34] *Ibid.*, p. 31, lines 140 and 144.

[35] *Ibid.*, p. 40, lines, 323-325.

[36] Jung, *CW* 16 § 534. Also his statement: "[...] the individual is faced with the necessity of recognizing and accepting what is different and strange as a part of his own life, as a kind of 'also-I'" *CW* 8 § 764.

[37] Jung, *CW* 7 § 409.

In *Leaves of Grass* the poet vicariusly weighs in as the spokesperson of the I from the very first line, indeed from the very first word; "I celebrate myself,"[38] he ecstatically declares. That this I as which the poet speaks is inclusive of all others (and as we shall see, of everything else that comes within his purview) is clearly established in the lines that follow: "And what I assume you shall assume,/For every atom belonging to me as good belongs to you."[39] Complete in himself, if only by virtue of his being always already the speculative result of his absolute exposure to the world around him, or as he expresses this, of his being "undisguised and naked," "mad for it [all] to be in contact with me,"[40] Whitman, in these opening lines, while "loaf[ing] and invit[ing] [his] soul," meditatively "consider[s] a spear of summer grass."[41] Reading down the page and over onto the next ones, we soon come to realize the poetic significance of this far from merely contingent detail. Such spears or leaves of grass, as we are readily given to understand, are metaphoric of the soulful bounty of people and occupations, events and situations that the poet glories in throughout the whole of this long, one-hundred-and-twenty-page poem. Several pages later, when grass is mentioned again, the situation is one in which a child clutching a handful of it confronts the poet with the wonder-infused question, "What is the grass?" Responding at first from within the ordinarily prevailing, subject here/object there difference of consciousness, or as this might also be indicated, from the mundane, egoic, empirically-minded side of the psychological difference that is being opened at this juncture, Whitman (who is also universalized as a figure in the poem, its speculative protagonist) modestly acknowledges that he does not know any more than the child does. This acknowledgement, however, is also the recognition that the child's question, having the character of a mystery, is not to be shrugged off in a literal-minded, condescendingly adult manner.

---

[38] Whitman, *Leaves of Grass*, p. 25, line 1.
[39] *Ibid.*, p. 25, lines 2, 3.
[40] *Ibid.*, lines 11, 12.
[41] *Ibid.*, line 5.

Why, it can even be said that with this remark the soul side of the psychological difference has become prescient, even as, having tarried with the negative by admitting that he does not know, Whitman is then able to allow himself as poetic I to vicariusly give the soul's answer to this question, if only by his adumbrating a series of extravagantly imaginative guesses.

> I guess it must be the flag of my disposition, out of hopeful green
>   stuff woven.

> Or I guess it is the handkerchief of the Lord,
> A scented gift and remembrancer designedly dropped,
> Bearing the owner's name someway in the corners, that we may see
>   and remark, and say Whose?

> Or, I guess the grass is itself a child …. the produced babe of the
>   vegetation.

> Or, I guess it is a uniform hieroglyphic,
> And it means, Sprouting alike in broad zones and narrow zones,
> Growing among black folks as among white,
> Kanuck, Tuckahoe, Congressman, Cuff, I give them the same, I
>   receive them the same.

> And now it seems to be the beautiful uncut hair of graves.[42]

Following upon the last of these lines, Whitman further imagines the vast variety of men and women whose grassy hair, sprouting out through the ground, shows that "to die is different from what anyone supposed, and luckier."[43] In another line he likens the grass pushing up through the ground to "so many uttering tongues!"[44] Clearly, the reader of Whitman is traipsing through soul country with him. From the single leaf of grass he had contemplated at the outset of his poem, via the handful of grass the child had asked about a few pages later, Whitman presents the American soul as a

---

[42] *Ibid.*, p. 29-30, lines 91-101.
[43] *Ibid.*, p. 30, line 121.
[44] *Ibid.*, line 110.

great continent-spanning grassland comprised of the endless abundance of sights that he exuberantly lists. Abstracting a bit, the import of this is that in Whitman's poetry a leaf of grass is the wonder that it is because *in its truth* it is the return from the otherness of all that it is not, just as, when considered from the vantage point that it *as this* sublatedly and sublatingly offers, the same can be said— and in poetry is said—of everything else that the poet in such I-quickening lyrical moments is simultaneously penetrated by and lavishes himself upon. Prosaically summarized, the point to be grasped is that, like the philosopher's stone of the alchemists, which was "known by a thousand names,"[45] grass in Whitman's treatment is the mutually-mediating, and thereby (inter-)subjectivity-creating soul that is common to all that for a people is. Again, just as Adam said to Eve when coupling with her, "bone of my bone, flesh of my flesh," so Whitman says to all that he sees and celebrates himself as, or in the otherness of, *grass of my grass*, if I may put it this way, vicariusly speaking on his behalf.

Saying the subjectivity of the substance seen

Other aspects of our topic are in the offing. In the sections that follow, we shall discuss the advent of the I from states of somatic, affective, and imagistic alienation, the me and my psychology fallacy, the I at the crossroads, and a whole lot more besides. But before we get to these topics, let us linger a while longer with Whitman.

In Part One of this essay, Giegerich's adage about what first appears in front of consciousness being the seed of what wants to become a new form of consciousness at large was cited. As contemplated by Whitman, the spear of grass that inspires his poetic vision is clearly indicative of this. Although first appearing as a mere object or content of consciousness, it is through his speculatively

---

[45] Jung: "The lapis that signifies God become man or man become God 'has a thousand names.'" *CW* 9ii, § 284. "The *prima materia* is […] cheap as dirt and can be had everywhere, only nobody knows it; it is as vague and evasive as the lapis that is to be produced from it; it has a 'thousand names.'" *CW* 13 § 209.

consorting with it as with his own other that the tautegorically-
apperceptive I of the poem is enabled to behold the American soul
more broadly, or rather, not merely to behold it in this way from
without, but to know it as such from within and to give voice to it
from that standpoint by saying I.[46]

> In all people I see myself, none more and not one a barleycorn less,
> And the good or bad I say of myself I say of them.
>
> And I know I am solid and sound,
> To me the converging objects of the universe perpetually flow,
> All are written to me, and I must get what the writing means.[47]

In other lines Whitman declares that "Not a youngster is taken
for larceny, but I go too and am tried and sentenced," and again that,
"Not a cholera patient lies at the last gasp, but I also lie at the last
gasp [...].["48] And so it is that he can vicariusly "speak the password
primeval,"[49] as he brilliantly calls it, the soul of the people as I.

Many more examples of the poetic I speaking as *vicarius animae* could
be cited from the pages of Whitman's great poem. And this is to say
nothing of the further lines and stanzas that may be added to the poem
from the scenes of life that the psychotherapist may witness in his
practice and speak up for in Whitman-like moments of speculative
insight. It only remains for my purpose here (which is to cultivate the
sensibility and boldness of the therapist in this regard) to cite a few
more passages from Whitman that I think especially pertinent.

---

[46] My reference to what I call the "tautegorically-apperceptive I" stems from
Giegerich's discussion of "the 'tautological' presupposition of myth interpretation."
This interpretive presupposition disciplines our reading of psychic images and
psychological situations in such a way that we are bound to take all of their details
as the mutually-mediating moments of a single truth. "[...] every essential detail
in a given myth is the selfsame *Notion of soul*, and the Notion of soul alone [...]
displays itself with its different determinations, with the different 'moments' of its
internal logic." Giegerich, *The Soul's Logical Life*, p. 121, pp. 119-123.

[47] Whitman, *Leaves of Grass*, p. 43, lines 401-405.

[48] *Ibid.*, p. 68, lines 949-950.

[49] *Ibid.*, p. 48, line 507.

But first a little personal context. Many years ago, when I was starting out, a supervisor of mine set me the challenge of limiting myself to making only a single utterance in each session. Also, during those early years, this time in the context of family therapy training, another supervisor advised me to "just let it all wash over you." By this he meant to resist the tendency to make sense of things too quickly, but rather to allow oneself to go under into the material of the session, even to drown in it at first on the prospect of gaining one's gills thereby. Putting these recommendations together we get to the idea of an interpretive comment in which the unity of the unity and difference of all the moments of the patient's situation achieve expression in the form of subject via the analyst's vicarius I-statement. Now with this in mind let us look at the first of my final citations from Whitman.

It will be recalled that grass for Whitman, whether contemplated as an individual spear, by the handful, or as a vast continent-spanning field or landscape, is indicative of the soul. Early in his *Leaves of Grass*, his I-saying, self-celebrating poetic reverie reflects the great diversity of the American soul in the image of a hay-wagon and barn loaded with grass and hay:

> The big doors of the country-barn stand open and ready,
> The dried grass of the harvest-time loads the slow-drawn wagon,
> The clear light plays on the brown gray and green intertinged,
> The armfuls are packed in the sagging mow:
> I am there ... I help .... I came stretched atop the load,
> I felt its soft jolts .... one leg reclined on the other,
> I jumped from the crossbeams, and seize the clover and timothy,
> And roll head over heels, and tangle my hair full of wisps.[50]

Precious about this passage, so reminiscent of the Christian hymn, "Bringing in the Sheaves," is the ready impression it gives of the I as the speculative result of the poet's exposure to all that has been seen, experienced, and claimed for his poem. Using my earlier expression, we could say that the poet has allowed all that he has

---

[50] *Ibid.*, p. 32, lines 160-167.

catalogued in his verses to wash over him, as it were. But no, the image is more precise than that. In *Leaves of Grass* the poet in his role of transcendental apperceptive I is depicted as "stretched atop the load" of hay. It is as if all that he has witnessed has produced him as its harvest-hand even as it now bears him along to the storage barn of his great poem. Why, there is even a somersault wherein his hair becomes at one with these wisps of harvested grass. A fitting halo this, for a consciousness become self-conscious by virtue of its meeting itself in the form of its other(s), or again, of the substance of the American soul coming to know itself also as subject. And here we may be put in mind of the speculative proposition (Hegel), wherein what is predicated of the subject (i.e., all that the poet sees and glories in) is not regarded as falling outside the subject as something inessential, extraneous, or merely additional, but is allowed to come home to the subject in a subject-seconding, essence-redefining manner.[51]

It only remains for the poet, or in our context the therapist, to give the wagonload of grass that he is borne along by the form of its being the sublatedness of all that he—its conscious, knowing apex—has resulted from, which of course is also to say, the form of subject. Significantly, Whitman characterizes this self-constituting, consciousness-realizing articulateness as a life and death necessity wherein the whole man is challenged to utter himself forth by giving voice to what is. "Dazzling and tremendous how quick the sunrise would kill me,/If I could not now and always send sunrise out of me."[52] A moment later he adds, "My voice goes after what my eyes cannot reach,/With the twirl of my tongue I encompass worlds and volumes of worlds."[53] And then there is this:

Speech is the twin of my vision …. it is unequal to measure itself.

It provokes me forever,

---

[51] We shall return to the topic of the "speculative proposition" in Part Three.
[52] Whitman, *Leaves of Grass*, p. 50, lines 562-563.
[53] *Ibid*, lines 566-567.

> It says sarcastically, Walt, you understand enough …. why don't you
>   let it out then?[54]

"Why don't you let it out …?" declares the soul to the poet, egging him on to be its vicarius spokesperson. And vicariusly chiming in, we can say to him as well, "having learned to be silent,[55] why don't you "speak the password primeval" on behalf of all that has drawn your attention, allowing it thereby to know itself through you as you do the same through it?"

And so it goes. Speaking as the soul that speaks through him from whatever and whomever he celebrates himself in the otherness of, Whitman declares:

> It is you talking just as much as myself …. I act as the tongue of you,
> It was tied in your mouth …. in mine it begins to be loosened.[56]

Again, as we have repeatedly seen, it is in this spirit, this voice, that Whitman compiles the many catalogues of sight poems that make up his *Leaves of Grass*.

> Neither a servant nor a master am I,
> I take no sooner a large price than a small price …. I will have my
>   own whoever enjoys me,
> I will be even with you, and you shall be even with me.
>
> If you are a workman or workwoman I stand nigh as the nighest that
>   works in the same shop,
> If you bestow gifts on your brother or dearest friend, I demand as
>   good as your brother and dearest friends,
> If your lover or husband or wife is welcome by day or night, I must
>   be personally as welcome;
> If you become degraded or ill, then I will become so for your sake;

---

[54] *Ibid,*, pp. 50-51, lines 568-570.

[55] Whitman begins a long tribute to listening, "I think I will do nothing for a long time but listen, and accrue what I hear into myself …. and let sound contribute to me." *Leaves of Grass,* p. 51, line 584.

[56] *Ibid.*, p. 82, lines 1244-1245.

> If you remember your foolish and outlawed deeds, do you think I
> cannot remember my foolish and outlawed deeds?[57]

The I that the poet gives voice to, here and in similar passages, is
the further determination of all that he identities himself with even
as, at the same time, all that he encounters in this speculative manner
provides the occasion for the distillate subject or I to reconfigure
itself more inclusively.[58] When, for example, Whitman encounters a
beautiful strong stallion, he briefly extols its various features and
imagines riding around on it for a time. But then, surmounting this
poetic moment, he leaves the stallion as some thing in front of him
behind, so as to continue his sojourn by means of a subtler mount
than it had sensually provided:

> I but use you a moment and then I resign you stallion ... and do not
>   need your paces, and outgallop them,
> And myself as I stand or sit pass faster than you.
> Swift wind! Space! My Soul! Now I know it is true what I guessed at;
> What I guessed when I loafed on the grass,
> What I guessed while I lay alone in my bed ... and again as I walked
>   the beach under the paling stars of the morning.[59]
> [...]
> I am afoot with my vision.[60]

In this passage, the poetic I's giving voice to itself is the result or
further determination of the image of the stallion's having been
"interiorized into itself." Said another way, in these lines the
Whitmanian-I comes into its own as "the return from the otherness"
of the stallion. Or to put it another way still, we can say that "afoot

---

[57] *Ibid.*, pp. 87-88, lines 13-28.

[58] It is interesting to note that Whitman occasionally inverted a sentence, placing
the I at the end of a phrase (e.g., "No dainty affettuoso I"). Although awkward to
the ear, and thus considered by some critics as one of the poet's bad habits, we
get a further hint from this about the I in Whitman's poetry having the character
of a speculative result. See the Whitman, *Leaves of Grass*, "Editor's Introduction,"
pp. xxix-xxx.

[59] *Ibid.,* pp. 56-57, lines 707-711.

[60] *Ibid.*, p. 57, line 714.

with [its] vision," the poet's I speculatively catches up with itself by means of a "leap after the throw" dialectic wherein what psychology's idea of projection ordinarily involves is radically reconceptualized in the light of an ancient sport in which the thrower of a large rock completes his throw by leaping after it.[61] And it is the same across the board, with every figure, every spear of grass, in which Whitman contemplates the American soul and brings it to self-consciousness.

> What the rebel said gaily adjusting his throat to the rope-noose,
> What the savage at the stump, his eye-sockets empty, his mouth
>   spiriting whoops and defiance,
> What stills the traveller come to the vaults at Mount Vernon,
> What sobers the Brooklyn boy as he looks down the shores of the
>   Wallabout and remembers the prison ships,
> What burnt the gums of the redcoat at Saratoga when he surrendered
>   his brigades,
> These become mine and me every one, and they are but little,
> I become as much more as I like.[62]

Reading these lines, the impression might arise of the poet becoming inflated by an omnivorous and merely self-edifying self experience. Indeed, in the line immediately preceding these, the poetic subject cries out, "O Christ! My fit is mastering me!"[63] It is crucial to realize, however, that throughout the poem the Whitman figure is offering himself to be used and surpassed just as he used and surpassed the stallion and all the many other figures populating its pages. As readers, too, we are meant to "use [the poem's robust, first-person plural protagonist] a moment and then resign [him]," just as he bids his interlocutors within the poem to do. For just as the Whitmanian I could as readily meet himself in each of us holding his book in our hands, lengthening it accordingly, so, it is equally implied, can we meet ourselves in Whitman and even outloaf and outgallop him.

---

[61] Wolfgang Giegerich, "The Leap After the Throw: On 'Catching up With' Projections and the Origin of Psychology," *CEP* I, pp. 69-96.

[62] Whitman, *Leaves of Grass*, p. 67, lines 933-940.

[63] *Ibid.*, line 933.

[...] each man and each woman of you I lead to a knoll,
My left hand hooks you round the waist,
My right hand points to the landscapes of continents, and a plain
    public road.

Not I, nor any one else can travel that road for you,
You must travel it for yourself. [64]

The poet of the I would have us jump over his checker. He would
have us travel in the manner he has exemplified, bringing the world
about us to consciousness by summoning up the temerity to say I.

Shoulder your duds, and I will mine, and let us hasten forth;
Wonderful cities and free nations we shall fetch as we go.

If you tire, give me both burdens, and rest the chuff of your hand on
    my hip,
And in due time you shall repay the same service to me;
For after we start we never lie by again. [65]

In another line he states,

You are also asking me questions, and I hear you;
I answer that I cannot answer .... You must find out for yourself. [66]

And in another,

Long have you timidly waded, holding a plank by the shore,
Now I will you to be a bold swimmer,
To jump off in the midst of the sea, and rise again and nod to me and
    shout, and laughingly dash with your hair. [67]

After pages and pages of doing it for us, the poetic I encourages the
reading I to vigorously come forward on its own responsibility.

---

[64] *Ibid.*, p. 80, lines 1204-1208.
[65] *Ibid.*, lines 1212-1216.
[66] *Ibid.*, line 1220.
[67] *Ibid.*, p. 81, lines 1229-1230.

Demurring slightly, subtracting himself, he brings push to shove such that the reader is forced to realize (leaving the self-identical stance of the ego behind) that he, too, can celebrate himself in the other in that way that at the same time imparts to the other the form of self. It is a matter "of going all in," as we like to say, a matter of "going for broke." Whitman's example of this inspiring the same passion for poetic apperception in the reader. In psychotherapy, the parallel of this is the way that the therapist's (not immediate, but eventual) boldness in giving voice to the patient's soul situation conducts to the same vocational boldness on the part of the patient. Having repeatedly witnessed the therapist daring to be as the Daniel of whatever his, the patient's, lion's den might be, the patient may find that he is able to do the same, and this with perhaps an even greater veracity.

The reluctant second advent of the I

So far, we have heard Jung and Whitman giving robust utterance to the I that "the we" in their time was, even as, the other way around, we heard the I of their day give robust utterance to itself through each of them. From Hegel as well we heard the I in strong voice. But what about that I, which despite its being logically achieved in the course of our common history, has subtracted itself from itself. The mumbling I? The mute I?

I raise this question with our work as analysts and psychotherapists in mind. It is often the case with our patients that to a lesser or greater extent, in one context or another, they have disavowed the subjectivity they exist as, retreated from the fullness and responsibility of their being I. This shows in their lagging behind the steps they have taken in life, the developments that have factually occurred, reluctant to let these to be true. At another level of description, it can be seen as an anxious or blasé tendency to shrink back from the selfhood that has been bequeathed to us as linguistic subjects from what Giegerich with the whole sweep of our Western cultural history in mind has called the historical emergence of the I.[68] Subtracting itself from itself, as I put it a moment ago, reversing its provenance, the I, instead of coming forward in its present circumstances and giving voice to itself as the comprehension of these, regressively disowns itself back into such precursive powers and principalities, gods and kings, as it is able to bow down before and hole up in itself beneath. Of course, in this connection we may readily think of the celebrity trendsetters, thought leaders, ideologues, and pundits of our times. But our self-divestment into these is only a part of what I have in mind here. Our erstwhile grovelling before gods and kings long after their historical demise can also have the form of our suffering from psychic and psychosomatic disorders. For, indeed, in our day, as Jung observed, with the soul's tendency to cling to former shapes of itself in mind, "The gods have become diseases; Zeus no longer rul[ing] Olympus but rather the solar plexus, and produc[ing] curious specimens for the doctor's consulting room [...]."[69]

The point I am driving at has to do with our tendency to demur with respect to the concept we exist as, the I we already are. Or again, with our reluctance to enunciate ourselves as such. Repeatedly throughout the course of our lives, now at this juncture and now at that, we may find ourselves subject to the vicissitudes of what may be called an already/not yet dialectic. Although we are *already* I, inasmuch as the form of the I has long been linguistically and conceptually achieved in the greater history of the soul, we may at the same time *not yet* effectively be I in that we have yet to declare as much in our particular situation and circumstances. Thinking a bit further about the complexity of this, we could say that it is not

---

[68] Wolfgang Giegerich, The Historical Emergence of the I: Essays about One Chapter in the History of the Soul (London, Ontario: Dusk Owl Books, 2020).

[69] Jung, *CW* 13 § 54. Continuing to succumb to this atavistic tendency on the heels having diagnosed it, Jung declares, "It is not a matter of indifference whether one calls something a 'mania' or a 'god'. To serve a mania is detestable and undignified, but to serve a god is full of meaning and promise because it is an act of submission to a higher, invisible, and spiritual being" (§ 55). Problematic here is indulging in gods when consciousness, mindedness, "the soul" has in the course of its history obtained the form of subject.

merely, as the adage puts it, that "you [i.e., the I that you are] have to already be there to get there." For while this is true it is only glibly so if we don't take into account that it is just as true that your *not* being there is a function of your implicitly already being there, which is why I referred earlier to the I's subtraction of itself from itself.— And in this connection, we may think by way of illustration of Parsifal's having so readily, indeed almost immediately, gotten to the Grail castle, only to then lose the grail due to his not asking the fateful, or better, destiny-embracing question, "Who does the grail serve?", which is as much as to say, "Who am I that this mystery has been shown to me?"

Now with these allusions and reflections in mind, let us look from another angle at what I am calling the reluctant second advent of the I. In her classic paper, "'Slouching towards Bethlehem …' or thinking the unthinkable in psychoanalysis,"[70] Nina Coltart discusses how painful psychic contents that have been dissociated into the body may, in the course of analytic treatment, gradually come to be tolerated as mental contents and articulated as feelings, thoughts, and insights. Extending her discussion, it may further be surmised that the I that in these forms is on its way is at the same time already established, enough, at least, to have defensively pushed these contents away. Likewise, in *The Soul's Logical Life*, Giegerich points to the same clinical referents, discussing the form-changes that these may pass through in terms of the concept of sublation, as this pertains to the logical movement of the psychic process from implicitness to explicitness.

> Generalizing the underlying conceptions [involved] with the help of HEGEL's philosophical language we could say: A psychosomatic symptom is "in itself" or, as it were, unbeknownst to itself, emotion (or, it is implicit, latent emotion); it is not "for itself" emotion, not explicitly or manifestly so (it is *ansichseiend*, not *fürsichseiend*, emotion). And emotion is *ansichseiend* (or latent) image; image is *ansichseiend* (or latent) Notion. Conversely, Notion is *sublated* (*aufgehoben*) image; image is *sublated*

---

[70] Nina Coltart's article in Gregorio Kohon, ed., *The British School of Psychoanalysis: The Independent Tradition* (London: Free Association Books, 1986), pp. 185-199.

emotion, emotion is *sublated* (interiorized, psychologized) behaviour or physical condition.[71]

We need to read this passage in terms of its author's related contention that "the soul always thinks,"[72] on the one hand, and his writings tracing the previously mentioned historical emergence of the I, on the other. Constantly thinking itself, the always thinking soul can have the form of a bodily symptom, an affect, an emotion, or image. And further to this, its thinking process can navigate across these substantiated proto-expressions of itself, obtaining, at a higher level of development, a form in which its thought character has become explicit. I would only add that the capstone to this (and as I use this word I think as well of "the stone of the wise," the *lapis* or Philosopher's Stone) is the notion I. Anticipating itself in the form of bodily and psychic expressions, the subject that these various determinations have all along implicitly been becomes explicit as I. Now I say "implicitly" and "all along" because the already, but not yet dialectic, which articulates itself across the range of psychic and somatic expressions of itself, is nested in the greater history of the soul's logical life. Indicative of Modernity is the realized subjectivity of the modern subject. Where once there had been God and the gods, Kings and the various roles that Tradition had demanded of its duty-bound subjects, now there is the modern subject, the more or less, or better, already, but not yet, sovereign

---

[71] Giegerich, *The Soul's Logical Life*, p. 48. Giegerich reminds us in his next paragraph of Jung's use of the spectrum analogy with respect to what he called the psychoid nature of the archetype. According to Jung, the same psychic content that has expressed itself in grossly unconscious and bodily ways at the infrared end of the spectrum may, at the more conscious ultraviolet end, come to be expressed via mental imagery and thought (*CW* 8 § 384ff). Along the same lines, I am reminded of Jung's paper, "Association, Dream, Hysterical Symptom," in which it is shown that a psychic content or complex that has appeared as a disturbed reaction in the word association experiment can also manifest itself as a hysterical symptom in the body and as a personified figure in a dream (*CW* 2 § 858-862).

[72] *Ibid.*, p. 124.

individual, reluctant as he may be to be that, hesitant as he may be to come forward as I.

Now with respect to such hesitancy and reluctance it is important to allow these their rights to be so. The patient must not be pressured to come forward, exhorted to say I. Respecting the "not yet" of his "already" existing as I, the therapist will bear in mind that had Parsifal in the Grail Castle at the beginning of that legend asked the decisive question, rather than failing to do so, there would have been no story. The adventures and calamities that subsequently tested his mettle, even as they eventually led him back to the grail enriched by such experiences, would not have been undertaken. The I, likewise, would be just a vacuous self-identical I without the mediating errancy that brings it down from its abstract ideality as a universal form to its particular and singularly lived reality as truly existing concept. The dialectic here, it may be added, is like the one that Samuel Beckett attests to in his novella, *Worstward Ho!*: "Ever tried. Ever failed. No matter. Try again. Fail again. Fail better." It is by learning in the face of thwarting negations to "Fail better" that a truth that had been known only in external and substantial terms is known also from within, that is, as subject, too. Always already, but not yet, the subject, the I, must again and again lose itself to find itself. And further to this, the analogy that suggests itself is that of the tempering process that makes a sword to be strong. But whereas an actual sword is first physically fashioned and only then in an additional step tempered, here with the provenance of the I it is more a matter of its tempering itself forth in the first place via the negations it again and again produces itself by negating.

A moment ago, with reference to what I called an already, but not yet dialectic, I spoke of the importance of respecting the patient's reluctance to say I. In keeping with this, it should additionally be mentioned that there are times when the therapist's speaking in the first person vicarius is only done silently. Cognizant of the fact that the I that we all are has long established itself in the course of our greater collective history, the therapist mediates the "already" side of the already/not yet dialectic via silent interpretations of the patient's soul situation, cognizant as he does so that the "not yet" side of the dialectic, mediated by the problems and symptoms the patient suffers, is what ensures that the I that finally arises, if arise it does, has its veracity, authenticity, and truth in being the immanent depth and sublated result of the patient's here and now. To illustrate this, let us imagine that the conversation between the patient and therapist has been rollicking along. At various points in their exchange it then happens, however, that while simultaneously concentrating on discerning the soul dimension of the material being discussed the therapist neglects or elects not to volley back the topic of the conversation. Slipping in this way off his end of the I-that-is-a-we/we-that-is-an-I teetertotter, the therapist allows the onus of thinking from the soul side of the psychological difference to shift to the patient. Whereas until this point it had been more or less exclusively the therapist who, being soulfully rooted in the form of the concept, had listened to the material being discussed in a tautological and tautegorical manner, now it may happen that the patient finds himself doing so. Why, it may even happen that, giving the unity of the unity and the difference of all that he has become cognizant of in this way the form of subject, the form of I, he may venture to say his truth.

The I at the crossroads of the symptom and setting

In the previous sections what Jung called the "coming to consciousness of the psychic process" was depicted in two very different ways. On the one hand, drawing upon Jung's self-experience while gazing over the Athi plains in East Africa, Hegel's reference to "the night of the world," and Whitman's poetically rendered scenes of American life, I presented the psyche as a landscape in which the I, like some latter-day Adam of that first landscape, the Eden of biblical myth, gives rise to itself as the subject of what *is* and name-giver of the same. It will also be recalled that in this connection, Jung's reference to the psychologist leaving laboratory and study behind to wander with a human heart through the world was quoted. And, of course, dreams belong to this type of depiction as well, since they for the most part are settings and landscapes in which the soul-as-I ever and again produces itself as the logically negative, sublated result of the various negations it has self-otheringly out-pictured itself as and self-productively challenged itself by.[73] On the other hand, drawing upon Coltart and Giegerich, the aforementioned "coming to consciousness of the psychic process" was depicted in terms of a movement from somatic/affective "thorn of the flesh" forms of implicit or retracted subjectivity to a more cognitive, linguistic, and articulated form wherein, leaving such symptomatic precursors of itself beneath itself, the I comes fully forward, as it may now be added, into the firing-line of one of the settings and landscapes mentioned above (!), there explicitly to state—and be!—its truth.[74]

Now, of course, it may not be obvious to the patient that what he apperceives outwardly as his situation or landscape and inwardly as affects, bodily symptoms, moods and anxiety states are alike in being but different ways for presenting the experience that consciousness has of itself in the course of its becoming conscious of itself, self-conscious. Having little or no access to the ego-transcending, truth-discerning, form of the concept, he will tend to experience them as external to each other, wholly different spheres. Which is why it may fall to the therapist as *vicarius animae* to interpretively give utterance to their unity, that is, to the truth that they variously reflect.

And how is the therapist to perform this mediating function? Well, imagine, if you will, that Jung's concept of the psychoid nature of the archetype did not merely have the form of a spectrum, as in his analogy for this,[75] but of a snake, and not just of any snake, but

---

[73] Again, with respect to "self-othering," Jung's reference to our "meet[ing] ourselves [...] in a thousand disguises on the path of life" is pertinent. For, be it in dreams or in soulful encounters in life, the I is the unity of itself and its other, even as Hegel writes that truth of personality is the return from other personalities.

[74] I should not imply that this is a one-way street. The I can also equivocate, demur, or go fully into retreat.

[75] Jung, *CW* 8 § 384, § 414.

of the uroboric serpent that bites and devours its tail even as it gives birth to itself from its own mouth. On the one end of this snake are the somatic expressions of psychic life that Jung saw as belonging to the infrared end of the psychoid spectrum, on the other, the imaginary, ideational, landscape and dreamscape-envisioning expressions that he assigned to that spectrum's ultraviolet end. Now, with this mix of analogies in mind, the task of the therapist can be characterized as one of speaking from any of the various moments of the total material presented as if from that one all-encircling point where the serpent's mouth and tail pass into and arise out of each other, and this, moreover, such that the various moments of the whole vicariusly achieve conceptual expression as I. For just as truth is the identity or conceptual unity of the identity and difference of such moments (Hegel), so is the I the identity or conceptual unity of the identity and difference of the settings and landscapes, affects, emotions, and psychosomatic symptoms, which (to put it in terms of a distinction of Aristotle's) are but the "accidents" (in the sense of features and composite qualities) of the soulful, conceptual substance which is its constituting and self-establishing task to be as the thinking and naming of.[76]

In an earlier section I mentioned that the philosopher's stone of the alchemists was known by a thousand names. Likewise, with respect to what I am attempting to convey in this section, it is important to add that there are as many ways to express the speculative unity of the differing psychic and somatic ways soul apperceptively displays itself and comes home to itself as there are dreams and life situations. Reflecting upon these at this juncture, I

---

[76] Putting this the other way around, we can also say that below the *niveau* of the tail-eating serpent, which, of course, is emblematic of the form of the concept, the form of the soul, the spectrum-spanning landscape/psychosomatics difference reflects the already, but not yet I's diremption of itself into these. And here, bringing yet another analogy into the mix, we can think as well of how a bead of mercury can both break itself apart into smaller beads and leap back together again into its oneness. Vicariusly stating the I of the patient and his situation, the therapist in a manner comparable speaks from the inflection point where one becomes many and the many, one.

find that numerous passages from our literature come to mind, and, along with these, some of the things I have been inspired likewise to say to my patients, as for example when, with Jung's emphasis upon the soulful character of the patients' present situations in mind, I have chided them about their "rubbing their toe in the back of their pantleg" whilst hesitating before and feeling daunted by their versions of the situations and landscapes that Deleuze and Parnet had in mind when, drawing upon Jung, they offered that the unconscious is structured in the manner of a landscape.[77] And this is to say nothing about the self-inflicted wounds of the deserter hoping to be carried away from the front.

The first passage to be mentioned is a text from the second-century Gnostic writer, Monoïmos, that Jung cites in his *Aion: Researches into the Phenomenology of the Self*:

> Seek him from out thyself, and learn who it is that taketh possession of everything in thee, saying: *my* god, *my* spirit, *my* understanding, *my* soul, *my* body; and learn whence is sorrow and joy, and love and hate, and waking though one would not, and sleeping though one would not, and getting angry though one would not, and falling in love though one would not. And if thou shouldst closely investigate these things, thou wilt find Him in thyself, the One and the Many, like to that little point ..., for it is in thee that he hath his origin and his deliverance.[78]

Pertinent in our context is the way that in this text the latency of the subject in the psychic and psychosomatic process is conveyed. Although the soul in this passage still has the form of God, expression of itself in the form of I is making its advent. As Monoïmos advises, if symptoms such as sleep disturbances and

---

[77] In his essay, "Doubling Back: Psychoanalytical Theory and the Perverse Return to Jungian Space," Kris Pint notes, "For Deleuze and Parnet the unconscious is not structured like a language, but rather like a landscape." In their words: 'The analysis of the unconscious should be a geography rather than a history.'"
https://www.academia.edu/2016126/Doubling_Back_Psychoanalytical_Literary_T heory_and_the_Perverse_Return_to_Jungian_Space? (accessed 4 January 2023).

[78] Jung, *CW* 9ii, § 347.

affects such as anger, sorrow, love, and joy are considered reflectively "thou wilt find Him in thyself, the One and the Many, like to that little point ..." The key words here are "in thyself." And in the line above this, key also is the use of the first-person possessive. Using an expression not unlike the negation-reckoning one that Christ cried out on the cross ("My God, My God, why hast thou forsaken me?"), the implicitly human subject, advises Monoïmos, need only say "*my* god, *my* spirit, *my* understanding, *my* soul, *my* body" when afflicted or innervated in these ways to become fully and explicitly so, the italicized "my" of this utterance being the way the I makes its appearance.

But what about the world around us, the apperceptive surround? Our text from Monoïmos needs to be supplemented with statements mindful of this dimension of the soul.

First among these is a statement Jung liked to cite from the alchemist Sendivogius: "*Maior autem animae [pars] extra corpus est,*" which we can translate to say, "the larger part of the soul, however, is outside the body."[79] Now with this in mind, many texts of Jung's may be cited in which what might variously be called the world-like, landscape-like, or *mise-en-scène*-like character of the psyche or soul is emphasized. Extrapolating beyond the laboratory setting of the Burghölzli Psychiatric Clinic where in his earlier years he investigated the feeling-toned complexes of his patients via the word association experiment, Jung writes in an early paper that "Everyday life is at bottom an extensive and greatly varied association experiment; in principle we react in one as we do in the other."[80] While surely this is true, more acute statements followed. Pushing off from the subject here/object there laboratory mentality and from the complexes of the patient's inner into a more fulsome sense of what he meant by the psyche or soul, he declares in a later statement that "As I see it, the psyche is a world in which the ego is contained."[81] Making much the

---

[79] Cited by Jung in his 12 July 1951 letter to Karl Kerényi, Jung, *Letters*, vol. 2, p. 19. See also Jung, *CW* 12 § 396, 399.

[80] Jung *CW* 4 § 700.

[81] Jung, *CW* 13 § 75.

same point, in a letter to a correspondent he wrote, "You rightly emphasize that man in my view is enclosed in *the* psyche (not in *his* psyche)."[82] And in another strong statement, Jung avers that

> [...] the collective unconscious is anything but an incapsulated personal system; it is sheer objectivity, as wide as the world and open to all the world. There I am the object of every subject, in complete reversal of my ordinary consciousness, where I am always the subject that has an object. There I am utterly one with the world, so much a part of it that I forget all too easily who I really am. "Lost in oneself" is a good way of describing this state. But this self is the world, if only a consciousness could see it. That is why we must know who we are.[83]

Psychologically, the difference between the self-identical I of "ordinary consciousness," on the one hand, and the I that only comes as the result of its world being reflected into itself,[84] on the other, is crucial. Thinking about the latter of these, I am reminded of a poet's having noted that when he is in a field he is the absence of the field, and, further to this, that wherever he is he is what is missing—or rather, not "he," but as he actually writes in his poem, "I." I am what is missing.[85] It is important to realize that the I referred to here only exists as its being that which is missing. Far from being literally missing, not there in any sense at all, the I is the subtle excess of what is there, consciousness as negative presence. And it is this, moreover, in the manner of the distinction Hegel drew when, clarifying what he meant by sublation, he insisted that while "Nothing is *immediate*; what is sublated [...] is the result of *mediation*; it is a nonbeing but as a result which had its origin in a being. It still

---

[82] 14 May 1950, Letter to Joseph Goldbrunner. Jung, *Letters,* Vol. 1, p. 556.

[83] Jung, *CW* 9i, § 46.

[84] For a discussion of "the soul's self-relation [as] a relation between itself as experiencing subject and itself as this subject's world" see Giegerich, *The Historical Emergence of the I*, pp. 18-19. Also of note is Jung's statement "The self could be characterized as a kind of compensation of the conflict between inside and outside" (*CW* 7 § 404).

[85] Mark Strand, *Selected Poems*, "Keeping Things Whole" (New York: Alfred A. Knopf, 1996), p. 10.

has, therefore, *in itself* the *determinateness from which it originates*."[86] Like Jung gazing out over the Athi plains, Whitman beholding each of the many scenes of American life, and Hegel expounding upon the "night of the world," I is the sublatedness of all that it is not, the distilled determinate negation of all that it out-pictures itself as,[87] which is also to say, the speculative surplus of its looking at its looking, *ad infinitum*.[88]

Now while bearing in mind the inspiring references and analogies I have just quoted from Jung, let us briefly consider some passages from Giegerich that serve in complimentary fashion the cultivation of the analyst's capacity for speculative insight and for the making of vicarius I-statements.

In the first of these passages, Giegerich boldly declares that "Truth […] is the world of life as it really happens to be plus the determined presence of man, his entrance into, and logical self-exposure to life."[89] Important to grasp in this statement is that "man" is no more taken for granted as existing beforehand than truth is. Like the truth he comes to know, man's constitution as man is ever and again the result of the wholehearted exposure of what *is* to itself in the medium of his species' capacity for mindedness.[90] Just as we learned from Aristotle that if the eye were an animal vision would be its soul, so now we may additionally learn that what may variously be called the soul, essential whatness, and truth of man lies in his seeking and knowing the soul, essential whatness, and truth of what *is,* which is why Aristotle defined man as the animal *with logos.* In our times, however, retreating from his essence as this, defaulting on his concept, man has largely gone

---

[86] G. W. F. Hegel, *The Science of Logic*, A. V. Miller, trans. (New York: Humanity Books, 1969), p. 107. This text has been dubbed "Hegel's speculative remark."

[87] Compare Jung's reference on p. 71 above to the "sheer objectivity, as wide as the world and open to all the world" that one is "lost in oneself" in.

[88] We already heard from Hegel that "what I look at is in me – for it is I, after all, who look at it; it is *my* looking," and further to this about how "Spirit steps out of this looking, and looks at its looking […]." For the full passage see p. 42 above.

[89] Giegerich, *The Soul's Logical Life,* p. 225.

[90] While it is true that the human being in the sense of the human animal already exists, this is to be understood as an aspect of the given world. It is, thus, merely an exposure condition to the production of Man and Truth.

truant with respect to this self-constituting call to come forward and expose himself—hence the seeming truthlessness of our so-called post-truth age. As Giegerich writes,

> The absence of truth in the modern world is the indication that man has absconded from the world (even while factually still being there). He does not want to show presence anymore. He stays out of it. He wants to live his life *as if* he were not really here. He has defined himself as absentee and wants to acquire knowledge *as* an absentee (the objectivism of the sciences and ontologism in philosophy are signs of the absenteeism of us humans). When life or fate knocks at his door, he says, 'nobody home.' Today, there is nobody there any more who could say to his (or our collective) real situation, "This is it!," "This is where Truth, where God must show itself."[91]

In psychology and psychotherapy, too, it may be added, this same self-subtraction and absenteeism everywhere prevails. Addressing this dimension of the topic in a related passage, Giegerich highlights the dissociation that is at play in what he aptly calls "usual psychology's idea of 'the human being who *has* such and such a psychology.'"

> The first obvious problem is the separation that occurs with this idea. We have the human being on one side and his psychology on the other. The form of the statement […] holds the one who has this psychology apart from the psychology he has. The person and his psychology are conceived as two independent realities. The word 'has' separates the two realities; even though it also combines them, it nevertheless does not undo the prior separation. Logically, the relation between these two distinct realities is set up more or less like the relation between a person and his clothes. What is actually one, is split apart, or dissociated." [Regarded in this way], *as* an existing being who has such and such traits and behaviour, [one is] 'inevitably immuniz[ed] … against his own psychology. He then *is* not, and cannot *be*, his psychology.[92]

---

[91] Giegerich, *The Soul's Logical Life*, pp. 224-225.

[92] *Ibid.,* p. 129. With respect to Giegerich's analogy to the external relation between a person and his clothes, if we contrast this with those dreams in which the dreamer or dream-I appears naked, might the interpretative possibility be

And is also not I, we might add!

Putting a finer point on the above analysis, Giegerich continues:

> A psychology whose subject of study is people's psychologies studies the life of the soul only to the extent that it has already gone through the ego and its mode of apperception, we could also say to the extent that the soul's life has already been prepossessed by the ego as '*its* psychology,' the psychology that I *have* (my puer psychology, my mother complex, my masochism, etc.), while the essential question what the *who* is that this is the psychology *of*, has been systematically left out.[93]

And what is the "who" from which psychology has dissociated itself? The answer could not be closer at hand: psychology itself in the sense of the soul as I. But while this is so, it is very commonly the case that in his reluctance to be self the patient places the psychology he construes himself as having out in front of himself as a shield, which is why it may fall to the therapist to bridge the dissociation with vicarius I-statements spoken on the patient's behalf out of the fullness of the situation he finds himself in.

---

considered that what the soul is insisting upon is the logical self-exposure to what is? Clothes, though only by contrast to this, could likewise be interpreted as a reflection, not just of what Jung conceptualized as the persona, but of the dream-I's equivocating, reserving itself. And here we may think of how after eating from the tree of the knowledge of good and evil, Adam and Eve covered themselves, ashamed of their nakedness.

[93] *Ibid.*, p, 132.

Part Three

SOME FURTHER ASPECTS OF THE VICARIUS MEDIATION OF THE EXPERIENCE THAT CONSCIOUSNESS HAS HAD OF ITSELF

That I that is the expression of the experience consciousness has had of itself

Once again, we begin with a little review. Earlier in this essay, reference was made to Jung's recognition that since "no explanation of the psychic can be anything other than the living process of the psyche itself," "psychology inevitably merges with the psychic process ... It can no longer be distinguished from the latter, and so turns into it." Continuing, Jung then crucially added, "the effect of this is that the process attains to consciousness." And further to this, that "psychology actualizes the unconscious urge to consciousness. It is, in fact, the coming to consciousness of the psychic process, but it is not, in the deeper sense, an explanation of this process [...]."[1]

What is true of psychology is true as well of the interpretive statements we are concerned with in these pages. Leaving the externality of explanation and of the application of existing theories behind, the therapist's saying "I" in the place of the patient (his soliloquizing, as were, out of the patient's *mise-en-scène*) is also a matter of "the coming to consciousness of the psychic process itself." For when an I-statement is formulated in the sense intended

---

[1] Jung, *CW* 8 § 429.

here, its utterance is the *result* of the psychic material's, subject matter's, or soul situation's further determination of itself, its giving voice to itself as an essence, an insight, a truth.

Now, while continuing to bear in mind this, Jung's presentation of the psychological difference as the difference between explanation, on the one hand, and the recognition, on the other, that far from being that, what may have been proposed as such is nothing more and nothing less than the further unfolding of the psychic process (its negative surplus, as it were!), I would now like to mention, apropos of this, Hegel's having characterized his *Phenomenology of Spirit* with the phrase, "the science of the experience of consciousness."[2] To be noted here is that the emphasis in this early version of that book's title is not upon the experience that some subject in addition to being itself has had of some object or external other, but upon the experience that that consciousness, which the opposites just mentioned exist as and have in common with each other, recursively, reflexively, determinately has had of itself. And this, I submit, is what psychology (i.e., the form of the soul as psychology) is about and what, on a much smaller scale, the psychotherapist gives voice to when enunciating vicarius I-statements.

I say "on a smaller scale" because, whereas for Hegel the science of the experience of consciousness had ultimately to do with the provenance of reason and freedom out of the world historical process through which these gave rise to themselves,[3] and while

---

[2] The phrase "Wissenschaft der Erfahrung des Bewusstseins" [Science of the Experience of Consciousness] appears on the title page of the First Part of the original edition of Hegel's *Phenomenology of Spirit*. Cf. *Phänonenologie des Geistes*, 6th ed. (Hamburg: F. Meiner, 1952), p. 61.

[3] In *Phenomenology of Spirit* what is meant by "the science of the experience of consciousness" is exemplified by Hegel's account of how consciousness in the form of empirically immediate Sense-Certainty is doomed to discover that it cannot state what it claims to know without recourse to the mediating input of the universals of language. When, for example, it attempts to indicate what it is aware of with the word "this," it finds that, since everything can be indicated with that word, it must on top of saying "this" resort to pointing as well. Learning from its experience of this negation, consciousness then acquires a new shape, that of Perception, and when this in its turn experiences its inner contradiction, consciousness as Perception gives way to consciousness as Force and Understanding. And so it goes. Continuing his far-ranging account of the self-transforming experience that consciousness has of itself during the course of its

afterhours, so to speak, in its scholar's study, psychology may likewise delve into what it calls "the soul's logical life,"[4] when it is a matter of work in the consulting room, the science of the experience of consciousness has to do with the provenance of truthful I-statements out of successive soul-situations that have for the patient moment-of-truth character. And here, with these resonances between Jung and Hegel in mind, I am prompted to recall the following statement of the Hegel scholar, J. N. Findlay:

> The action of thought is to *negate* the basis from which it starts, to show it up as not being self-subsistent, and so to have in it a springboard from which it can ascend to what is truly self-subsistent and self-explanatory.[5]

In our context, it is by negating any basis in external explanations and reductive interpretations that psychology ascends to a form of itself that is "truly self-subsistent and self-explanatory," truly psychological, truly I. Put another way, it is by pushing off (or as Giegerich would say, by having already pushed off[6]) from the ordinarily prevailing subject here/object there difference of consciousness, that thought makes good on its negatively-aspiring bid to produce that subject or I-statement that is as the voicing of what may variously be called "the heart," "the soul," "the essence" of the initially apperceived, but not yet fully reflected into itself, substance or situation. Distributed to the one and to the other side of this (as

---

history, Hegel further shows how consciousness in the shape of Stoicism gives way to consciousness in the shape of Skepticism, and how this in turn gives way via further experiences of determinate negation to other shapes, such as that of the Christian religion, etc. Likewise, in another of his books, *The Science of Logic,* what is meant by the science of the experience of consciousness can be grasped by following how Hegel is led by his thinking the concept Being to speak in the same breath of this being indistinguishable from Nothing and then to the resolving of this contradiction with the notion, Becoming.

[4] Wolfgang Giegerich, "Psychology—The Study of the Soul's Logical Life," *CEP* IV, pp, 325-350.

[5] John N. Findlay, "Foreword," In G.W.F. Hegel, *Hegel's Logic: Being Part One of the Encyclopedia of Philosophical Sciences*, William Wallace, trans. (Oxford: Claredon Press, 1982).

[6] For a discussion of the dialectic of pushing off see Giegerich, *CEP* vol. II, p. 233.

we have learned to call it, horizontal) difference, there is, to begin with, the therapist on the one hand and the patient on the other, or again, the patient on the one hand, his situation on the other. But psychology begins with the negation of this positive basis and horizontal difference. Its version of "the science of the experience of consciousness" with the verticality-establishing opening-up of the psychological difference.[7]

To illustrate what I am attempting to convey here, let us contrast the experiences that people have when they come before the law and the experience that the law has of itself during the process of its being tested in the situations and circumstances upon which it must render its verdicts. No doubt, the people involved in court proceedings have all kinds of experiences. There are the experiences their case is about and that they present their versions of to the court and, along with these, the experiences and feelings they have about the immediate situation of having to appear in court to do so. But the greater subject of the proceeding is "the Law" itself. It is *its* experience of itself in the matter at hand, the science of the experience of *its* consciousness in the situation being adjudicated, that the court preceding is about. Often, of course, the Law has little to report on in this regard. Its already established values are merely applied to the situations brought before it in a routine, mechanical way and in the manner of the aforementioned external, subject here/object there relation. It is not, in these instances, reflexively thrown back upon itself by the matter at hand. At other times, however, the particularity of the human situation that the court proceeding is about shows up a deficiency in

---

[7] Introduced by Giegerich, the term "psychological difference" has to do with a psychological standpoint that distinguishes between the soul and the human being. According to the perspective established with this distinction, a truly *psychological* psychology must take "the soul" as its principal subject matter and resist the tendency to reduce its phenomenology to human beings in the manner of the personalistic psychologies. "For a true psychology, only the soul, which is certainly undemonstrable, merely 'metaphorical' and for this reason a seeming nothing, can be the 'substrate' and subject of the phenomena. The human being is then their object; he or she is nothing but the place where soul shows itself, just like the world is the place where man shows himself and becomes active. We therefore must shift our standpoint away from 'the human person' to the 'soul.' (N.B.: I am talking of a shift of *our standpoint, perspective, or of the idea in terms of which we study, just as before the concrete experience of individuals and peoples.*) Giegerich, *CEP* I, p. 115.

the previously established law, and out of this—call it the law's experience of itself—an entirely new ruling arises. Why, it even happens that sometimes a new determination of the law, a new precedent, is set.[8]

Now, while keeping in mind this illustration of what "the science of the experience of consciousness" looks like in a court of law, let us return to psychotherapy. There, too, it is again the case that we are not so much concerned with the thoughts and feelings that at once both make for and are given to explain the experiences the patient has had on a personal, ego level (though, of course, our interest and empathy may be shown to him in these regards), but with the truth of those thoughts, the veracity and justness of those feelings.[9] For it is often the case with us humans that we will endure, and even indulge in, any amount of suffering, if only to forestall a treasured conviction or precious ideal from being shown to be untrue.[10] Our cure, by contrast, belongs to the soul-side, the allocuting I-side, of the psychological difference. It is a matter of the truth-producing, insight-quickening experience consciousness has of itself when, having been sworn in, as it were, its psychic and ego-psychological claims are weighed against themselves as against a feather in the matter at hand.

Giving the talking cure the form of the speculative sentence

An analogy used by Hegel to convey the dialectical character of the thinking process that, in matters great and small, "the science of the experience of consciousness" involves and consists in is helpful as well for our purpose here of cultivating in the psychotherapist the capacity to give voice to the experience (not that the patient has, but) that the consciousness or concept that the patient exists as and is subject to (both consciously and unconsciously) has had of itself

---

[8] For a fuller discussion of the law as the other of psychotherapy and analysis see my *Psychology's Dream of the Courtroom* (New Orleans: Spring Journal Books, 2016). Subsequently published by Routledge, 2020.

[9] Cf. Giegerich, *The Soul's Logical Life*, pp. 214, 229.

[10] A point discussed by Giegerich in *The Soul's Logical Life*, pp. 228-229. See also Jung's statement, "Neurosis is always a substitute for legitimate suffering" (*CW* 11 § 129).

through him. In the early pages of his *Phenomenology of Spirit*, Hegel discusses the laborious conceptualizing and reconceptualizing effort that the reading of difficult texts requires. Especially when reading works of philosophy, it regularly happens that by the time we get to the end of an important sentence we can no longer recall what the subject of the sentence is and so must go back over it again, perhaps several times, to grasp this in the light of its predicate. Of course, sometimes the problem has merely to do with the poor quality of the writing. The sentence is unclear and we have to edit as we go. But the kind of sentences Hegel draws to our attention—"speculative sentences," as these have come to be called—though not straightforward, are by no means faulty or badly written. Rather, they are ones that must be gone over *thinkingly* in order to be understood, their meaning being a function of our coming to realize, during the course of our going over them again and again, that the information stated in the predicate is not something additional or external to the presumptive subject of the sentence, but the subject reiterated in different terms, the subject a second time. Reading and re-reading, perhaps many times, we find with such sentences that our initial understanding of what they are about is changed-up, reflexively redefined, via the way this first impression is mirrored in its predicate.

> We learn by experience that we meant something other than we meant to mean; and this correction of our meaning compels our knowing to go back to the proposition, and understand it in some other way. [11]

And again:

> Thinking [...] loses the firm objective basis it had in the subject when, in the predicate, it is thrown back on to the subject, and when, in the predicate, it does not return into itself, but into the subject of the content. [12]

Now, what Hegel describes in these passages by means of his analogy to reading is descriptive as well of the listening process in

---

[11] Hegel, *PhS*, § 63, p. 39.
[12] *Ibid.*, § 62, p, 39.

which analytic psychotherapists are engaged. As analysts and therapists we routinely find that in addition to establishing and maintaining a straightforward conversational rapport, we must at the same time go over the statements, dreams, and life situations of our patients again and again, inwardizing these into themselves such the experience consciousness has had of itself (which is also to say, "the coming to consciousness of the psychic process," or again, "the soul's speaking of itself"[13]) can be vicariusly accessed and interpretively conveyed.

A few simple examples come readily to my mind. In one of his sessions, a patient who was something of a perpetual student, obtaining multiple degrees as a way of extending the tenure of his provisional life,[14] told me of a thought he had had after attending a presentation about the rich career possibilities that were open to him due to a qualification he had recently earned. "I can go anywhere," he ventured to declare, surprised as he did so to hear himself admit to being on the brink of real prospects. Listening to these words, I was as struck as he was by the robustness of their tone. Repeating them inwardly to myself, reading and reading, it seemed to me that the reference in the predicate to being able "to go anywhere" could be heard as reflexively imparting itself to the sentence subject, i.e., to my patient's "I," changing up the meaning of what his utterance of this meant, this in the manner of a speculative sentence. Heard in this way, the tail-end of his statement, the part about being able to "go anywhere," was not merely indicative of a possible prospect, something that in addition to being himself he could also do. On the contrary, it was already indictive of, performative of, a new determination of himself, a new I, as it were. To highlight this, I then said his words again out loud a few times, progressing as I did so from expressing them in the manner of an ordinary sentence ending in a mere quality predicate, to an expression that allowed his sentence's last words to be heard, teeth in tail, as an essential predicate redounding uroborically upon the subject. Understarting what was meant, I first enunciated his sentence to say "I [*in addition to being who I literally, positivistically, self-identically, already am*] can go anywhere," and then via a different intonation allowed its speculative meaning to

---

[13] Jung, *Gesammelte Werke* 9i, § 400, see: Giegerich *The Soul's Logical Life*, p. 123.

[14] H. Godwin, Baynes, "The Provisional life," *Spring 63: A Journal of Archetype and Culture* (Woodstock, CT. Spring Journal, 1998), pp. 55-72.

boldly resound: "*I [am he, the one who]* can go anywhere!" He in his personhood, as first-person perspective, as self, was now *that.* Just as traditionally, in times of old, American Indians had names such as "Shadow-That-Comes-In-Sight" or "Old Lodge Skins" (I had been reminded as we spoke of these characters in the novel, *Little Big Man*[15]), so was the patient now "I-Can-Go-Anywhere."

My second example is that of a man who told me in one of his sessions about a woman he had been friends with during his university days. Although back at that time (it was a dozen years ago now) he had had a romantic interest in her, he did not make this known to her, or even fully to himself, but rather allowed himself to be inhibited by the thought that he did not stand a chance with her. But now, years later, in the aftermath of a failed marriage, and for reasons pertinent to his therapy, he found himself recalling this earlier love interest. "I loved that woman," he emphatically declared, surprised as he did so to be saying this so boldly. From his tone as I listened, I knew that he was telling the truth. But was it not too late for that? Too late for the truth? By no means. It is never too late for that. Never too late for a relationship or life situation to receive its speculative (re)reading. Now, of course, I am putting it this way in order to reflect my patient's story in the analogy to reading that Hegel used in his discussion of the speculative sentence. Back when he was first attracted to his woman friend, my patient's reading of the challenge this confronted him with had been as straightforward as it had been inhibiting and literalistic. Effacing the passion he was galvanized by, deserting its call, he conducted himself as if he as subject was nothing but a self-identical positivity who, in addition to being that, had only an external relation to his desire, on the one hand, and to the woman he was smitten with, on the other. But the experience that consciousness had had of itself, but which he had back then not allowed to be true, had nothing to do with anything as objectual as that. On the contrary, as the precipitate of a love episode he'd not been up to at the time, it even then, as he haplessly and ineffectually tarried with that, had rather to do with a subject-to-subject, I-to-I relation wherein what it means to be I is a function of the mutual fast-influencings of one's being recognized and reflected into oneself by a partner who is also I. We already cited

---

[15] Thomas Berger, *Little Big Man* (New York: Dial Press, 1964). Also, the film by the same title, Arthur Penn, director, Cinema Center Films, 1970.

Hegel's reference to self-consciousness and spirit as "an 'I' that is a 'We' and a 'We' that is an 'I'."[16] My patient's "I loved that woman" caught my ear as having the same speculative structure. In enunciating these words, he was finally recognizing, finally owning up to the fact, that he was not merely himself in the sense of the abstract subjectivity we evasively reduce ourselves to when we point to ourselves and say "who, me?," but himself in the acutely ethical sense of a subject who knows— eye to eye and I to I—that he is being regarded and counted on as such by another who, knowing the same, is also an ethical subject.[17]

"I loved that woman!" Just as in the previous example, I repeated out loud my patient's statement about being able to go anywhere in such a way that my intonation highlighted its speculative sense, so again in the present case with this sentence. Saying it back to him in the manner of a salutation, I recognized him as being in essential regards the return from the otherness of the woman he had finally owned up to having loved, supporting in this way his actualization as a personality adapted to his truth. And, here, my putting it this way, brings to mind Hegel's teaching that "as far as personality is concerned, it is the character of the person, the subject, to surrender its isolation and separateness." "Ethical life," he continues,

> love, means precisely the giving up of particularity, of particular personality, and its extension to universality—so, too, with

---

[16] Hegel, *PhS*, § 177, p. 110.

[17] It is because we human beings are creatures "capable of I contact," as Roger Scruton puts it, that we become constituted as persons and selves. "Self and other come into consciousness in a single act of recognition, which bestows on me the ability to know myself in the first person at the same time as demanding that I recognize the first-person being of you." What is more, what might be called the metaphysics of our personhood has its provenance in this subject to subject, I to I, relation of mutual dependency and responsibility. Scruton refers in this connection to the repertoire of emotions humans uniquely display: "indignation, resentment, and envy; admiration, commitment, and praise—all of which," he continues, "involve thought of others as accountable subjects, with rights and duties and a self-conscious vision of their future and their past." We only need to capitalize the emotions listed to highlight their aforementioned "metaphysical" character. Roger Scruton, *On Human Nature* (Princeton, N.J. & Oxford: Princeton University Press, 2017), pp. 36, 54, 25. With respect my comment on capitalizing the names of the emotions, I allude to Bachelard's call for "a psychology of capital letters." Gaston Bachelard, *The Poetics of Reverie*, D. Russel, trans. (Boston: Beacon, 1971), p.173.

'friendship.' In friendship and love I give up my abstract personality and thereby win it back as concrete. The truth of personality is found precisely in winning it back through this immersion, this being immersed in the other.[18]

Speculative reversal

I want to say a little more about the speculative sentence as a heuristic devise complimentary to an interpretive stance that would formulate interpretations in such a way that the topics and situations that are of concern to the patient may be given voice to by the analyst "as both substance and subject" (Hegel). In his "Psychological Commentary on 'The Tibetan Book of the Dead,'" Jung observes that what he there calls "the primacy of the psyche […] is the one thing that life does not make clear to us." This is so, he continues, because "We are so hemmed in by things which jostle and oppress [i.e., by the stuff of external predicates!—G.M.] that we never get a chance, in the midst of these 'given' things, to wonder by whom they are 'given.'"

> Perhaps it is not granted to many of us to see that the world is something "given." A great reversal of standpoint, calling for much sacrifice, is needed before we can see the world as 'given' by the very nature of the psyche. It is so much more straightforward, more dramatic, impressive, and therefore more convincing, to see all the things that happen to me than to observe how I make them happen. Indeed, the animal nature of man makes him resistant to seeing himself as the maker of his circumstances. That is why attempts of this kind were always the object of secret initiations, culminating as a rule in a figurative death which symbolized the total character of this reversal.[19]

---

[18] Hegel, *Lectures on the Philosophy of Religion*, One-Volume Edition, The Lectures of 1827, Peter C. Hodgson, ed., R.F. Brown, P.C. Hodgson, and J. M. Stewart, trans. (Berkeley: University of California Press, 1988), pp. 427-428.

[19] Jung, *CW* 11 § 841. Cited in our context, Jung's reference to "figurative death" can be read as descriptive of the transformative experiences that consciousness has of itself in the retort of whatever the situation or phenomenon may be that has quickened it forth. It may, thus, usefully be compared to Hegel's statement about, how, when "tarrying with the negative," the truth is known in "utter dismemberment." Hegel, *PhS*, § 32, p. 19.

Observing in what happens how *I* make it happen. A figurative death in which consciousness or the subject is initiated into a more acute determination of itself via a reversal of the ordinarily prevailing subject/external predicate relation. —The "I" Jung refers to in this text is produced by the inwardization of what *is* into itself, or as this may also be put, by the *thinking* of what *is* (which, of course, is something very different from merely thinking *about* what is).

In a relatable passage, Hegel states,

> What I have in my consciousness, that is for me. "I" is this void, this receptacle for anything and everything, for that which everything is and which preserves everything within itself. Everyone is a whole world of representations, which are buried in the night of the "I." Thus, "I" is the universal, in which abstraction is made from everything particular, but in which at the same time everything is present, though veiled. It is not merely abstract universality therefore, but universality that contains everything within itself. We start out using "I" in a wholly trivial manner, and it is only our philosophical inquiry that makes it a subject matter of inquiry. In the "I" we have thought present in its complete purity. Animals cannot say "I"; no, only man can do so, because he *is* thinking itself.[20]

Returning to Jung with all this in mind, I would now like to cite a teaching of his from the *Visions Seminars* that greatly extends the interpretive reach of the speculative mode of analytic thinking we have been discussing into all aspects of life and life experience.

> Of course, in a way nothing ever happens to you which you are not. The life you live is your life. All your experiences are yourself—that is exactly what you are. So when somebody complains that he has been a victim of a sexual attack, say, in early youth, and explains his whole life by that occurrence, one must say that it is lamentable, yet it was himself, he experienced it. You see, if such a thing had happened to him but it had not been his own experience, it would have made no impression; it would have passed him by. Usually neurotic patients think that one thing or another has had such and such an effect, but other people go

---

[20] Hegel (as per the *Zusätze*), *EL* § 24, p. 57.

through numbers of potentially devastating experiences that leave no impression because they are not theirs. Yet sometimes experiences are traumatic, and one has to be a mental acrobat to explain why—because a dog waggled his tail at one or something like that.[21]

"A dog waggled his tail at one or something like that." Regarded externally, what happens to us may seem a trifle. Why such a fuss, over such a little thing? Well, because sometimes what is contained in the predicate is not merely some external object or thing, but the "arrows and slings" of our happening to ourselves in a self-redefining way.[22] And this may be so even with happenings that are generally regarded as being traumatic, such as the sexual attack Jung mentioned. In these cases, too, session by session, over perhaps a longer course of therapy, a speculative appreciation of the I as the negation-negating result of its own devastating provenance may be in order.[23]

Getting serious

In the passage from Hegel that was quoted in the previous section, the observation was made that "We start out using 'I' in a wholly trivial manner, and it is only our philosophical inquiry that makes it a subject matter of inquiry." This statement is true as well when transposed into the context of our work with patients. Psychotherapy, too, starts out from utterances which, even when stated in the first person, are very often underdetermined, or as Hegel put it, "trivial." Listening to the patient, we often feel that he is not yet taking himself and the situation he is speaking about seriously. And we may feel this even when he is telling us something

---

[21] Jung, *Visions Seminars*, Book 1, p. 146.

[22] Here, I am leaving out of account occasions where an obsolete subjective stance uses the events befalling it neurotically to maintain its fixations. Regarding this problem see: Wolfgang Giegerich, *Neurosis: The Logic of a Metaphysical Illness* (New Orleans: Spring Journal Books, 2013).

[23] Here again, we can think of Hegel's "tarrying with the negative." Compare as well, Nietzsche's well-known statement: "*Out of life's school of war*. What does not destroy me, makes me stronger." Walter Kaufmann, *The Portable Nietzsche* (New York: Viking Press, 1954), p. 467.

that is difficult or grim. Even then, it is as if he is reserving himself as a subject, or as this may also be expressed, holding back from the experience that the consciousness he exists as has already (though, of course, only implicitly) had of itself through him. And this is so, moreover, even as at the same time it apperceptively out-pictures itself as his environing surround. Impressions, thoughts, and feelings, given out as mere reactions to associated life events, are described in a wholly external manner. I say "external" here because in essential regards the patient keeps himself out of the matter of which he is speaking. It is as if the situation he is speaking of were only a matter of his being impinged upon from without. Missing from his account is any indication of his having put himself at stake with respect to the question of whether the impressions, thoughts, and feelings he has expressed are true. He complains, but somehow manages to demur at the same time. He suffers, but in an externalizing way that forestalls his being reached (his *having already* been reached) by the critique that the consciousness he exists as has visited upon itself through him via the arrangement, in Alfred Adler's sense, of some fated comeuppance or happenstance. But now he is on the record, speaking to a therapist who takes him more seriously in what he says (or omits to say) than he takes himself. His predicates, or at least a key few of these, become self-(re)defining speculative predicates, if only because the therapist is listening. We could also say, his statements about this, that, and the other topic or thing speculatively disclose the I that he is as thinking itself (recall Hegel's putting it this way in the passage cited in the previous section) inasmuch as the therapist may be presumed by him to be that, too, a thinking subject with inwardness, and to be regarding him in kind.[24]

An old story from the early days of our analytic tradition well illustrates the seriousness-dialectic just described, wherein a person

---

[24] We already know that "for psychology there is no Other. Or the other that there is is 'the soul's own other, its internal other, itself *as* other." In the present context, let us recognize the double sense of this, wherein neither *what* is being talked about ("this, that, or the other thing"), nor *who* is being talked to (the therapist), are external to the patient, but rather speculative foils of the soul as self-relation, which is also to say, of the I that the patient as thinking is. Giegerich, et. al., *Dialectics and Analytical Psychology: The El Capitan Canyon Seminar* (New Orleans: Spring Journal Books, 2005), p. 26.

who has been languishing below the level of his achieved self-consciousness "pulls up his socks," as it were, when he realizes that he is being fathomed by another person, another subject. When he was serving as a test subject in an association experiment conducted by Jung, Jung's boss, Eugene Bleuler, showed little reaction when an allusion was made to a particular matter that he thought only he, and not Jung, knew about. But when subsequently Jung touched upon the matter again, this time in a way that let Bleuler know Jung was aware, Bleuler displayed deflections on the monitoring equipment indicative of a strong emotional reaction. As Jung recalling this incident years later put it, "When he is alone with himself, he does not know what value this affair has for him, or how much it bothers him. But when he knows that someone else knows about it, then he gets the actual affect."[25] It is important to grasp, with respect to our topic, that Bleuler's reaction is not simply a matter of personal embarrassment felt before Jung. While surely being that, more deeply comprehended, his emotional arousal and embarrassment was rather a matter of his sudden recognition of being weighed in the balance of a like-knows-like, or better, I-fathoms-I relation and found to be wanting—not merely by Jung as external other, but deeper than that, by himself within the ambit of his being, as we have heard repeatedly from Hegel, "an 'I' that is a 'We' and a 'We'

---

[25] W. Giegerich's translation of lines from Jung's "Über Gefühle und den Schatten. Winterthurer Fragestunden. Texbuch, Zürich and Düsseldorf 1999. For Giegerich's discussion of Jung's having drawn upon this incident concerning Bleuler to illustrate his observation (pertinent also to our topic here) that "we are strangely incapable of realizing our own feelings, that is, to notice […] the things that are of concern to us," see his *What Is Soul?* pp- 236-241. Without mentioning Bleuler, Jung briefly discussed the experiment he performed on him in another context: "There is a tremendous difference in the assumption of telling something and the actual telling of it, a fact which I was once able to test out experimentally. I told a man whom I was testing to think of something disagreeable, but to let it be something I did not know about. I took his electric resistance in the so-called psycho-galvanic experiment, and there was very little change. In some way I knew he was thinking about something very disagreeable that had happened that morning, but something which I had found out by accident, and of which he was confident I knew nothing. I said to him, 'Now I will tell you what the disagreeable thing was,' and as soon as I told him I got a tremendous reaction in the current." William McGuire, ed., *Analytical Psychology: Notes on the Seminar Given in 1928* (Princeton, N.J.: Princeton University Press, 1989), p. 46.

that is an 'I.'"[26] In the few sentences immediately above Hegel's observation about our usually starting out using I in a wholly trivial manner, it is explained that "'I' is the universal, in which abstraction is made from everything particular, but in which at the same time everything is present, though veiled. It is not merely abstract universality therefore, but universality that contains everything within itself"[27]—including oneself and one's interlocutors, we might add. What Hegel here describes is the logical form of the I. We could also say, the logical form of the true, essential, or as this was characterized earlier, serious subject. Now, in the incident we are discussing, it is shown that on this occasion Bleuler was not conducting himself as a subject in this full sense. What Jung would call a complex, Hegel a particular that has not been abstracted from (i.e., negated and sublated), tied him back to the psychic side of the psychological difference, while the other side of that difference, the soul side (corresponding to that I that constitutes itself as "thinking itself" via the inclusion of all that it has abstracted or differentiated itself from within itself[28]), fell to Jung as representative of Bleuler's own knowing-better to mediate, if only via his simple presence as likely being a subject in that sense, too.[29] Why, it was quite as if in

---

[26] Hegel, *PhS,* § 177, p. 110. With respect to embarrassment, it is interesting to note how this may sometimes be a matter of one's being hoist upon the psychological difference as upon one's own petard. In such moments as these, embarrassment is less about its human-all-to-human *content,* than about the *form* of the subject as subject. One is embarrassed because one's unconsciousness, thoughtlessness, and above all, one's not fully being the I that one actually and accountably is, has been placed on display.

[27] Hegel (as per the *Zusätze*), *EL* § 24, p. 57.

[28] Just as Hegel defined truth as the identity of identity and difference, so likewise may the I be defined—as an identity of identity and difference. As for Hegel's relatable teaching that the I is a universal that abstracts from every particular thing even as at the same time it sublatedly contains everything it has abstracted itself from within itself, it is important to include other subjects, other persons, in this formulation. They, too, rank among the things abstracted from and included, hence Hegel's reference to the I as also a We.

[29] It is notable that it is the experimental situation inclusive of Jung, not the association experiment alone, that shows that there is a content, or to use Hegel's word, a particular, that the test subject has not abstracted himself from and (re)integrated. And this, of course, has implications for the I. In the story Jung tells about Bleuler, evidence of the latter's ill-accordance with himself as I is thrown into relief within the prevailing transference. From this it can readily be

the situation described, Bleuler was suddenly hauled up, "like a guilty thing surprised,"[30] before the bar of his intersubjective universality as an I/We. And here, in this connection, I am further reminded of Jung's reference to occasions when the psychic process has the character of "as endless inner trial in which [the subject] is his own counsel and ruthless examiner."[31]

The self-productive wresting itself free of the I from the situations and occasions that anticipate and call it forth

"Without wishing it," writes Jung, "we human beings are placed in situations in which the great 'principles' entangle us in something, and God leaves it to us to find a way out."[32] Recalling this line at this juncture, I am led to wonder about its pertinence with respect to our topic in these pages. What other aspects of the soul as I, and of the vicarius mediation of this by the therapist, follow from this statement?

Above the door of his home in Küsnacht, Jung famously inscribed the words, "*Vocatus atque non vocatus deus aderit*"—"Called or not called, the God will be present." In keeping with this, throughout the vast corpus of his writings, Jung also made frequent reference to God, paying tribute in this way to the religious figuration of the soul that had preceded his "psychology 'with soul.'"[33] The sentence cited at the top of this section is an instance of this. God (or for us, the soul as God) is in it similarly presumed to be an abiding presence in our lives. But how, then, are we to understand the part of the sentence about God leaving it to us to

---

seen, as Jung put it many years later in his essay on the transference, "the soul cannot exist without its other side, which is always found in a 'You.' *CW* 16 § 454.

[30] William Wordsworth, "Ode: Intimations Of Immortality From Reflections On Early Childhood," line 149.

[31] Jung, *MDR*, p. 345.

[32] Jung, *CW* 10 § 869.

[33] Jung, *CW* 8 § 661, translation modified.

find a way out? Evidently, God does not only look out for the sparrow.[34] Withdrawing or absenting himself, he also makes us to be on our own, so as to fly on our own wings. Drawing upon a Hegelian term, we can see in this the action of a determinate negation. Determinate negations are negations that yield in their wake a speculative result, corresponding, as it were, to the earlier discussed "science of the experience of consciousness" (Hegel) and "coming to consciousness of the psychic process itself" (Jung). While, on the one hand, God is ever nigh in Jung's discourse, a constant reference throughout his life and writings,[35] on the other hand, Jung also held that "the present is a time of God's death and disappearance."[36] Taken together, what we have here is the unity of the unity and difference of the mutually contradicting moments of a soul-transforming self-negation wherein, subtracting itself from itself, but not entirely, the soul as God kenotically[37] imparts itself to the human subject via the aforementioned (p. 61) push-comes-to-shove dialectic, even as, declares Jung in a passage that came into my mind along with the previous ones I have cited, "The meaning of my existence is that life has addressed a question to me. Or, conversely, I am a question which is addressed to the world, and I must communicate my answer, for otherwise, I am dependent on

---

[34] Matt. 10:29.

[35] And in his practice, too, as the following statement indicates: "I make my patients understand that all the things which happen to them against their will are a superior force. They can call it God or devil, and that doesn't matter to me, as long as they realize that it is a superior force. God is nothing more than that superior force in our life. You can experience God every day." McGuire & Hull, eds., *C.G. Jung Speaking*, pp. 249-250.

[36] Jung, *CW* 11 § 149.

[37] My word here "kenotically" is derived from *kenōsis*, which is the theological term for God emptying himself of his divinity when in the form of Jesus he died on the cross. See *Phil.* 2:5-8: "Let this mind be in you, which was also in Christ Jesus: Who, being in the form of God, thought it not robbery to be equal with God: But made himself of no reputation, and took upon him the form of a servant, and was made in the likeness of men: And being found in fashion as a man, he humbled himself, and became obedient unto death, even the death of the cross."

the world's answer. That is the suprapersonal life task, which I accomplish only by effort and with difficulty."[38] Notice, here, the transformation from soul in the form of religion and God to soul in the form of psychology and the I that is exemplified in this statement. Referring to himself in the first-person singular, Jung does not look to God to provide the answer to the question of the meaning of his existence, but subject to the self-divesting, self-movement of the latter, recognizes that he as the subject that heir to this he *is* has at once both question and answer character—and this, moreover, in a still-vertical, though no longer upward-looking sense. Called or not called, the soul as I will bespeak itself—not, mind you, as subject in some abstract, isolated sense,[39] but as the unity of the unity and difference of the various moments of the situation in which the great principles, as Jung put it, have entangled us.

Why, it is quite as if the relation between the entanglements that God leaves us in, on the one hand, and our coming into our own as subjects by finding our way out of these, on the other, is like the relation of the Gordian Knot to the sword that cut it. The proviso here, however, is that this analogy is only apt if we do not think of it as an external relation of separate entities—an entanglement or knot here, a solution or sword there—, but as an involution of substance into subject, wherein the knot in our analogy is the sheath, the entanglement the scabbard, of the solution, sword or I that produces itself as the latter by drawing itself out of itself as the former.

---

[38] Jung, *MDR*, p. 318. Although this passage, as I have shown, is readily relatable to the idea of the modern subject as the sublated result of the going under of God, its actual context has to do with Jung's surmises with respect to the possibility that unanswered questions may have been passed down to us from previous lives, our own or those of our ancestors.

[39] Inasmuch as I, knowing others to also be I, speak out of the We that we thus intersubjectively are (and this, by the way, is what "reasoning" is), what I say in the first person singular is, at the same time as it is that, said by me in what may be called the first person universal.

And here I find that a few further references spring helpfully to mind from out of the night of the I. Writing with respect to the political revolutions of world history, Marx observes that "Mankind [...] inevitably sets itself only such tasks as it is able to solve, since closer examination will always show that the problem itself arises only when the material conditions for its solution are already present or at least in the course of formation!"[40] Surely, this statement rings true in our context as well. Very often, indeed most of the time, a similar claim can be made on the smaller scale of the individual. "Staged by the soul," his problems, too, be they personal, familial, societal, or cultural, apperceptively arise as the self-actualizing occasion or proving ground of his coming more fully into his own as "thinking itself" (Hegel), or to put it another way, as seriously thinking, seriously speaking, universalized I.[41] And following upon this, another line from Marx, which is applicable in our context, suggests itself: "a situation is created which makes all turning back impossible, and the conditions themselves call out: *Hic Rhodus, hic salta!*"[42]

Above, I placed Jung's line about God leaving it to us to find a way out of the archetypal situations in which we find ourselves in determinate sequence with his statement about the meaning of his existence residing in his sense that life addressed a question to him,

---

[40] Karl Marx, Preface to "A Contribution to the Critique of Political Economy." www.marxists.org/archive/marx/works/1859/critique-pol-economy/preface.htm (accessed 27 June 2022).

[41] My speaking here of happenings and situations that are "staged by the soul" and of challenges and problems that "apperceptively arise" is resonant with my earlier citation from Jung about the "reversal of standpoint [... that] is needed before we can see the world as 'given' by the very nature of the psyche." See p. 84 above. Compare as well, Jung's statement "everyday experience shows that it is quite possible for a superior, though subliminal, foreknowledge of fate to contrive some annoying incident for the sole purpose of bullying our Simple Simon of an ego-consciousness into the way he should go, which for sheer stupidity he would never have found by himself." (*CW* 9i, § 414)

[42] Cited from Karl Marx's *The Eighteen Brumaire of Louis Bonaparte.* www.marxists.org/archive/marx/works/1852/18th-brumaire/ch01.htm (accessed 25 December 2022).

even as he was a question addressed to the world. It only remains to connect this—let us call it, what Jung in this way had to offer with respect to the enlightened coming of age of the human subject in the wake of the religion that had preceded it—with the psychological stance of the psychotherapist in his role as *vicarius animae*. In a passage from his memoirs that sheds light upon this, Jung writes once again of his being confronted with questions, this time in the context of his analytic proclivity to speculatively apperceive psychotherapeutic situations as also having question character:

> As a doctor I constantly have to ask myself what kind of message the patient is bringing me. What does he mean to me? If he means nothing, I have no point of attack. The doctor is effective only when he himself is affected. 'Only the wounded physician heals.' But when the doctor wears his personality like a coat of armor, he has no effect. I take my patients seriously. Perhaps I am confronted with a problem just as much as them. It often happens that the patient is exactly the right plaster for the doctor's sore spot. Because this is so, difficult situations can arise for the doctor too—or rather, especially for the doctor.[43]

With this passage, and the whole of our discussion thus far in mind, let us cite what another of the students and patients who consulted Jung observed in this regard. We have already heard from Marvin Spiegelman about Jung's tendency to speak about himself in a way that was at the same time a "'speaking to my condition,' and addressing himself to all my problems, fears, concerns, and deep desires."[44] Concurring with this, we also heard from Jane Wheelwright about how Jung allowed himself to be equally affected by the issues she presented to him, relating to her in such a way that,

---

[43] Jung, *MDR*, p. 134. Notice that in the context Jung provides it, the adage he cites—about only the wounded physician being able to provide healing—does not indicate that the physician is wounded to begin with, though of course he may have his issues, but that the patient's situation and material affects him, cuts into him, infects and wounds him in that sense.

[44] Cited by John Haule, "Analyzing from the Self: An empirical phenomenology of the 'third' in analysis" in Roger Brooke, ed., *Pathways into the Jungian World: Phenomenology and Jungian Psychology* (London, New York: Routledge, 2000, p. 257).

as she put it, she "did not register on the difference of our statures!"[45]
Along the same lines, Aniela Jaffé writes,

> Sometimes I would come to an analytical hour filled with some
> difficulty, a dream or something else of importance, and burning
> to talk to Jung about it. But that was not to be. Jung himself was
> filled with something and would begin talking, and once he was
> well into his story he forgot the time. There was no stopping him.
> A good deal of strength was needed to interrupt him in sessions
> like these and to trot out one's own affair, which of course, he
> never took amiss. I never possessed the strength, and few others
> did either. But those who did not interrupt him found—regularly,
> I should say—that a surprise was in store for them. When once
> they were gripped by the torrent of thoughts, images and
> experiences, intuitions and dreams, amplifications and
> interpretations, once they swam along with it, without giving a
> thought to the advancing hand of the clock, they would suddenly
> discover that Jung's words were relating more and more clearly
> and finally with the greatest precision to the very thing that they
> had wanted to tell him about. They got the answer without having
> posed the question.[46]

Once again witness is given by an analysand of Jung's that the
interpretations he ventured, when serving in what I am calling the
soul-mediating, I-enunciating role of *vicarius animae*, had often the
form of providing answers as the whole man to questions that,
although not having been explicitly posed by the patient, were
nevertheless implicit within the universality that they as earnest
subjects shared and raised each other to within the ambit of the "'I'
that is a 'We' and ... 'We' that is an 'I'"[47] In a further comment, it is
noted by Jaffé that patients like her, who had been impressed by
such sessions with Jung, would sometimes remark on Jung's having
impressive powers of intuition. It is important to realize, however,
that while it is certainly not wrong to characterize Jung as being

---

[45] *Ibid.*, p. 258.

[46] Jaffé goes on to add, "Naturally, these sessions were exceptional; normally
Jung was the most patient and attentive of listeners." Aniela Jaffé, *From the Life
and Work of C.G. Jung*, R. F. C. Hull and Murray Stein, trans. (Einsiedeln: Daimon
Verlag, 1989), pp. 120-121.

[47] Hegel, *PhS*, § 177, p. 110.

intuitive, placing too great an emphasis on intuition (which, after all, was merely a *psychic* attribute of Jung as a person) shortchanges the *psychological* dimension of his interpretive work and is thus in default of the psychological difference. Better, I think, to surmise that in the sessions described Jung well knew that questions and contributions put to him by the patient would in all likelihood have been posed from the ego side (we could even say, from the patient side) of the psychological difference, that is, in the literalistic manner of external reflection. But the soul side of the psychological difference corresponds to Jung's statement about life addressing a question to him (as, indeed, it does to us all) even as he (and we) are a question addressed to the world.

A circle remains to be squared, a contradiction to be resolved, with respect to the question-character of life and selfhood we just heard about from Jung. In the passage I quoted from his memoirs, this shows in the fact that Jung only describes *himself* in this manner. The meaning of *his* existence is that life has put a question to *him*, even as *he* is a question put to the world. And along the same lines, this, as we discussed, is how he related to his patients—as mediators of questions having meaning for *him*. Surely, however, this claim of Jung's is not exclusive to him, but applies as well to his patients, students, and readers, too. Why, it may even be surmised that writing and practicing in a manner that invited identification (while being born of this at the same time), his speaking of himself and of his meaning in this way was once again an instance of his speaking for and as the other, for and as us all. It may therefore be said that for Jung the meaning of his existence was nothing isolated,[48] but had its truth in the universality of its coinciding with the meaning of ours as well. And this meaning, as we heard, is that life puts a question to *us* each even as *we* are a question put to the world.

But how is it then, given that the question-character of life and selfhood is as true for the patient as it is for the therapist,[49] that the robustness of the latter's grappling with the question that the patient's situation presents, does not have the deleterious effect of upstaging or outstripping the patient in this regard?

---

[48] Compare his statement, "Individuation does not shut one out from the world, but gathers the world to itself." *CW* 8 § 432.

[49] Perhaps, I should stipulate here: the Jungian patient and the Jungian therapist.

I will not go over again all that Jung learned from the association experiment he performed upon Bleuler, but will only recall his finding that the subject is only subject in the eminent sense as a function of his recognition that he is, or at any moment could be, known by another subject, another I. And so it is with regard to the question-character of *our* existence and meaning. This, too, no matter how personal the matter in question may be, also has a mutually-evoking, intersubjective valence. I to I, question mark to question mark: before the bar of that selfhood that is constituted by the mutual recognition of ourselves as selves, the meaning of our existence is that life presents a question to us, not, however, in our isolated, extra-linguist, abstract subjectivity (if there even be such a thing), but as the I that produces itself, answers for itself, as the negation-negating result of that "'I' that is a 'We' and … 'We' that is an 'I'"[50] that each of us in our highest determination *are*.

The subtly of the dialectic that is involved in what I am trying to get across in this section brings an old Jesuit maxim to mind. As formulated by Hevenesi, the maxim states that the first rule of action is to

> assume/believe that the success of your undertakings depends entirely on you, and in no way on God; but, nonetheless, [to] set to work as if God alone will do everything, and you yourself nothing.[51]

Thinking along similar lines (but adjusting for the difference that for us the transition from the soul having the form of God to its having the form of I has long since taken place), the question-character of the self and its therapy can be stated in a manner that sublates from the outset the false immediacy of its seeming to be distributed between the patient and therapist in accordance with the ordinarily prevailing difference of consciousness, subject (or therapist) here, object (or patient) there. As a possible wording of this, I offer the following:

> Conduct each session as if the questions presented by whatever the soul-situation may be that has of its own accord become topical are exclusively addressed to the therapist and up to him to

---

[50] Hegel, *PhS*, § 177, p. 110.

[51] Cited by Žižek in his *On Belief* (New York: Routledge, 2001), p. 125.

answer, believing at the same time, the other way around, that they are exclusively addressed to the patient and wholly his to answer.

As a formulation expressing the psychological standpoint, this maxim, I have found, helps to prevent even what may seem to be a very intense relationship between therapist and patient from eclipsing or obfuscating what Jung, alluding to what we call the psychological difference, referred to as "the great relationship."[52] In actual sessions, moreover, without ever needing to be overtly stated, the contradictory simultaneity it encourages provides for the therapist who bears it in mind, and increasingly his patient as well, to consider the questions posed them from their own and each other's vantage point, united as they do so in a deference, if I may call it that, to the soul as "the third of the two."[53]

Several passages from Jung may be cited here for the sake of the hints and impressions, life and nuance, they provide with respect to our topic, in general, and to my adaptation of the maxim from Hevenesi, in particular. In the first of these, Jung in a letter to James Kirsch opines:

> With regard to your patient, it is quite correct that her dreams are occasioned by you. The feminine mind is the earth waiting for the seed. That is the meaning of the transference. Always the more unconscious person gets spiritually fecundated by the more conscious one. Hence the guru in India. This is an age-old truth. As soon as certain patients come to me for treatment [i.e., to Jung specifically], the type of dream changes. In the deepest sense we all dream not *out of ourselves* but out of what lies *between us and the other*.[54]

---

[52] Jung, *CW* 10 § 367.

[53] Giegerich, "On the Neurosis of Psychology or the Third of the Two," *CEP* I, pp. 41-67. Cf. Jung's reference to the third of the two: "The elusive, deceptive, ever-changing content that possesses the patient like a demon now flits about from the patient to doctor and, as the third party in the alliance, continues its game, sometimes impish and teasing, sometimes really diabolical. The alchemists aptly personified it as the wily god of revelation, Hermes or Mercurius." *CW* 16 § 384.

[54] Jung, *Letters 1*, p. 172, to James Kirsch, 29.IX.1934. Jung's observation that the dreams of certain patients change when they come to consult him has been generally observed, as, for example, the saying "Freudians have Freudian dreams and Jungians have Jungian dreams" attests. See also Paul Kugler's discussion of

As regards this passage, I will only highlight the accordance of Jung's idea about dreams being occasioned by the analyst with his aforementioned statement about his having "constantly [...] to ask myself what kind of message the patient is bringing me. What does he mean to me?"[55] And now, further to this, let us set another of Jung's statements alongside these. Writing with respect to a hallucinatory schizophrenic patient in the Burghölzli, who had wanted to tell him about a vision he had had, Jung declares, "He wanted me to see it [too] and, being very dull, I could not see it. I thought, 'This man is crazy and I am normal and his vision should not bother me.' But it did. I asked myself: What does it mean? I was not satisfied that it was just crazy ..."[56] Here again, we have the therapist relating to the patient's material, not only on the patient's behalf, but as a challenge put to him in his, the therapist's own, substance and depth. But what about the other side of the maxim that I adapted, the part about the patient's having (while in the presence of another subject, another I!) to grapple, as it were, all on his own with the question posed by his soul situation? In this connection, I readily think of Jung's statement about his having

---

how an analyst's epistemological and ontological assumptions determine what comes true in the patient's treatment—his *Raids on the Unthinkable: Freudian and Jungian Psychoanalysis* (New Orleans: Spring Journal Books, 2005), pp. 85-1-7. For a discussion of the patient's resistance as a critique of the psychotherapist's theoretical commitments see my *The Dove in the Consulting Room: Hysteria and the Anima in Bollas and Jung* (Hove & New York: Brunner-Routledge, 2003), esp. pp. 96-118.

[55] Jung, *MDR*, p. 134. With this deceptively simple statement, the psychologist Jung establishes the field of endeavour we call psychology via an opening up of the subjective dimension of whatever the matter of interest may be that compels him to think in its terms. I take his statement in both an immediate and personal sense and in a more general and formal one. In the former sense, Jung indicates himself. Pointing at himself and saying "me," he is the subject. In the latter sense, by contrast (and here again we can mention the psychological difference), his reference to himself as "me" is not to be taken literally, but rather as a way of expressing the *form of subjectivity*, i.e., the form wherein—"bone of my bone, flesh of my flesh"—some matter of interest is interiorized into itself via being allowed to think itself out through "me."

[56] Jung, *CW* 18 § 85. For a throughgoing discussion of Jung's analytical attitude as reflected in this and similar statements and examples see W. Giegerich, *CEP* I, pp. 128-152.

learned from experience "that all coercion—be it suggestion, insinuation, or any other method of persuasion [...] ultimately proves to be nothing but an obstacle to the highest and most decisive experience of all, which is [for the patient] to be alone with his own self, or whatever else one chooses to call the objectivity of the psyche. The patient must be alone if he is to find out what it is that supports him when he can no longer support himself."[57] An important teaching. It may still be wondered, however, how bold interpretation on the therapist's part is to be squared with inviting the same from the patient. With respect to this, a few final lines. In the context of reporting on what he called his "indirect way of approach to the instinctual image," Jung describes how in his practice he would generally "try to give [his patients] provisional interpretations at least, so far as I was able, interspersing them with innumerable 'perhapses' and 'ifs' and 'buts' and never stepping beyond the picture laying before me. I always took good care to let the interpretation of each image trail off into a question whose answer was left to the free fantasy-activity of the patient."[58]

Science or art?

The question posed in the title of this section can readily be answered. Whatever the pretensions that Jung and the psychological tradition stemming from him may have or have had to being a science,[59] Jungian psychology is practiced as an art. Now, of course, when it comes to application the same may be said for several of the various disciplines of science. We speak, for example, of the medical arts and even of engineering arts. But in these contexts, a discipline is only an art in the sense of the Greek word *technē*. Little or no comparison is intended to art in the sense of the Arts and the Humanities. Jungian psychology, however, is different

---

[57] Jung, *CW* 12 § 32.

[58] Jung, *CW* 8 § 400.

[59] These are fully discussed by Sonu Shamdasani in his *Jung and the Making of Modern Psychology: The Dream of a Science* (Cambridge, U.K.: Cambridge University Press, 2003).

in this respect. While it, too, is practiced as a *technē*,[60] when we call it an art it is with an analogy to the creative and expressive arts in mind. Painting, sculpture, architecture, music, poetry, theatre and literature, etc.—these are not merely adjacent spheres of interest to which Jungian psychology and psychotherapy are externally related. On the contrary, as genres of the soul's speaking about itself,[61] they have for it the speculative, mirroring character of an internal other. Little wonder then that Jung, as he reports in his memoirs, should have had to have that conversation with the voice of a muse-like inner feminine figure in himself, later called "the anima," in which he contested over the question of whether his efforts to plumb the depths of the soul by working psychologically with his own dreams and fantasies was a science or an art. "What am I really doing?" Jung recalls having asked himself. "'Certainly this has nothing to do with science. But then what is it?' Whereupon a voice within me said, 'It is art'."[62]

I bring up this well-known and much discussed episode from Jung's biography, both for its pertinence with respect to our topic of the analyst as *vicarius animae*, and for the new light it can be seen in once its pertinence to this is shown in sufficient detail.

Carrying on with his account of this early encounter with the anima, we next hear from Jung that he was "astonished" by the claim which the feminine voice in him made. "It had never entered my head that what I was writing had any connection with art." Puzzled about this, he then had the thought, "'Perhaps my unconscious is forming a personality that is not me, but which is insisting on

---

[60] But here see Michael Whan's essay, "On the Nature of Practice," *Spring 1987: An Annual of Archetypal Psychology and Jungian Thought* (Dallas, TX: Spring Publications, 1987). Under the subheading "Against Technique," Whan discusses the ambivalence in the Jungian tradition to Jungian practice being subsumed under the concept of technique, this owing to its recognition of the personal equation. As Jung writes in a passage cited by Whan, "The personality of the patient demands the personality of the doctor and not artificial technical procedures" (p. 80).

[61] Jung, "In myths and fairytales, as in dreams, the soul speaks about itself, and the archetypes reveal themselves in their natural interplay, as 'formation, transformation / eternal Mind's recreation.'" Giegerich's translation of *Gesammelte Werke* 9i, § 400. Cited from his *The Soul's Logical Life*, p. 123. The poetic phrase quoted by Jung is from Goethe's *Faust* II.

[62] Jung, *MDR*, p. 185.

coming through to expression.' I knew for a certainty that the voice had come from a woman. I recognized it as the voice of a patient, a talented psychopath who had a strong transference to me. She had become a living figure in my mind."[63] It is with these last two lines that the connection to our topic shows. Just as the analyst in his or her role as *vicarius animae* will speak for the patient as if from the standpoint or perspective of his, the patient's *mise-en-scène*-born I, so Jung found that a voice in him "that is not me" was the voice of a patient with a strong transference to him. We have already heard from Jung about how as a doctor he always regarded his patients as posing a question or bringing a message that was as important for him as it was pressing for them. And in keeping with this, we have repeatedly heard from several of those who trained and analyzed with Jung of his uncanny ability to soliloquize about interests and topics of concern to him that at the same time touched deeply upon their issues and questions. Returning with all this in mind to Jung's account of his initial dialogue with the anima, we learn that when the woman's voice in him went silent in response to his having resistantly said back to her, "No it is not art! On the contrary it is nature," Jung's next thought was "that 'the woman within me' did not have the speech centers I had. And so I suggested that she use mine. She did so and came through with a long statement."[64]—So there we have it, the origin story, if I may call it that, of Jung's speaking for and as the patients in whom he had at the same time met himself (even as, at the same time, the soul came home to itself via the transferential dialectic of the "I that is a We and the We that is an I" within the staging ground of the consulting room).

It is noteworthy in our context how—refusing his muse, as it were[65]—Jung in this initial encounter, and again five decades later in his account of this in his memoirs, rejected the anima's suggestion that his psychological work on his fantasies had anything to do with art.

---

[63] Jung, *MDR*, p. 185. The meaning of the term "psychopath" as used by Jung in this instance has a different meaning than it has today. It refers to someone prone to nervous disorders due to what was then thought to be a hereditary taint.

[64] Jung, *MDR*, p. 186.

[65] A topic I explored in an early paper, "The Refusal of the Muse: Jung's Artist Complex and the Anima" 1983, unpublished.

What the anima said seemed to me full of a deep cunning. If I had taken these fantasies of the unconscious as art, they would have carried no more conviction than visual impressions, as if I were watching a movie. I would have felt no moral obligation to them. The anima might then have easily seduced me into believing that I was a misunderstood artist, and that my so-called artistic nature gave me the right to neglect reality. If I had followed her voice, she would in all probability have said to me one day, 'Do you imagine the nonsense you're engaged in is really art? Not a bit.' Thus the insinuations of the anima, the mouthpiece of the unconscious, can utterly destroy a man. In the final analysis the decisive factor is always consciousness, which can understand the manifestations of the unconscious and take up a position toward them.[66]

Striking about this passage is how resistant it shows Jung to have been to the speculative dimension of the psychic process he describes. Although the anima was an inner figure (associated, to be sure, with an actual patient of his[67]), he takes her literally, her inner otherness externally, and tightens up against the concept-expanding potential of the idea she suggests. The problem here was Jung's regarding what the voice within him said on an ego level, as if he as a person were its addressee. The topic of the inner dialogue, however, was not Jung the man, but psychology. In keeping with this, a stronger reading would regard the subject of the experience to be the *concept of psychology*, or to be more precise, the *concept of psychology or notion of soul that Jung as psychologist embodied and existed as.*[68] It would be this that the anima as speculative predicate determinately-negated with her identification of psychology with art. Or to put it another way, it was psychology in its abstract self-identity, not Jung, that was "utterly

---

[66] Jung, *MDR*, p. 187.

[67] Scholars and historians of analytical psychology have speculated about the identity of the patient referred to by Jung in this text. Kerr has suggested Sabina Spielrein, while Shamdasani has suggested Maria Moltzer. John Kerr, *A Most Dangerous Method*, (New York: Alfred A. Knoff, 1993), pp. 502-507. Sonu Shamdasani, "Memories, Dreams, Omissions," *Spring: A Journal of Archetype and Culture* 57, 1995, pp. 115-137.

[68] We are a far cry here from the common view, held even by many professional Jungians, of the anima as the feminine component of the personality that is to be integrated.

destroy[ed]," even as, holding its own against this (note the contrast, here, with Jung's having merely acted-out this "tarry[ing] with the negative" as a resistance on an ego level), psychology at the same time destroyed this destruction, achieving thereby a wider concept of itself in which the former difference between psychology and art was cancelled and overcome.

But, of course, despite all I have just shown, Jung *was* a psychologist in the higher speculative sense of that anima that in the encounter described had so rattled his cage. As we know from the course of his subsequent career, his concept of psychology *had* re-definitionally come home to itself via the return from the otherness of what the anima as internal other had asserted about psychology and art. And this applies to his stance as analyst, as well. Indeed, his functioning for his patients as *vicarius animae* (or as this now may also be put, *his having lent them his speech centres*, just as he had lent them to the figure of the anima in that early exchange with her) was clearly rooted in a speculative conception of psychology, that is, in a psychology conceived of as, and derived from, the experience that the definitions and concepts we exist as and live by have had of themselves through us.

Though Jung's understanding, as I have shown, even as late as his memoirs, lagged behind the self-othering episode with the anima he there describes, there are other texts in which he catches up with the speculative meaning of art as the other of psychology, itself a second time. Especially illustrative of this are his essays "Psychology and Literature" and "On the Relation of Analytical Psychology to Poetry." In these essays, if I may put it this way, Jung has a very much more congenial dialogue with the anima about the speculative identity of psychology and art than he had in the one recalled in his memoirs. And the upshot of this was that, against the foil of Freud's reductive and personalistic approach to psychology in general, and to the psychology of art and the artist in particular,[69] Jung's own prospective creative-synthetic approach to psychotherapy came

---

[69] Jung opines about Freud's reductive approach to art and psychology of the artist in the first half of "On the Relation of Analytical Psychology to Poetry." To be fair to Freud, it is important to know that he did acknowledge, on a least one occasion, that "before the problem of the creative artist analysis must, alas, lay down its arms." *S.E.* XXI, p. 177.

strongly to the fore.[70] To substantiate this claim, we need only listen for resonances between what he says in these essays with respect to the works of great artists, on the one hand, and the smaller scale consulting room equivalents of such statements as can be heard in the therapeutic speaking of the analytic psychotherapist, on the other. Touching on a few important instances of this, Giegerich has discussed the similarity between Jung's observation that "A poet or seer lends expression to the unspoken inner depth [or inner truth] of his time [*dem Unausgesprochenen der Zeitlage*]"[71] and Jung's own giving "expression to the unspoken truth that was constellated through the presence of the patient."[72] Similarly, and citing Jung again, Giegerich notes that "the 'poet voices the truth of all [everyone]',[73] which means: of nobody in particular, not even of himself, and yet (or precisely for that reason) of everyone. Completely subjective and for that very reason objective: absolute?"[74]—And here let me add that I can only agree with Giegerich's further reflections upon what I have written in the present essay:

> The artist [writes Jung] "is in the deepest sense an instrument and for that reason *beneath* his work …"[75] [In a way analogous to this] I think the I or subjectivity that you are concerned with [in Part One of the present essay] must somehow be seen in the light of the creative work: its subjectivity, its I. The Third of the Two is

---

[70] In a passage that shows the contribution of an aesthetics-inspired focus upon the art object itself to the formation of Jung's non-reductive, prospective approach to psychology, Jung writes: "Psychology and aesthetics will always have to turn to one another for help, and the one will not invalidate the other. It is an important principle of psychology that any given psychic material can be shown to derive from causal antecedents; it is a principle of aesthetics that a psychic product can be regarded as existing in and for itself. Whether the work of art or the artist himself is in question, both principles are valid in spite of their relativity." *CW* 15 § 135.

[71] Jung, *CW* 15 § 153, translation modified.

[72] Wolfgang Giegerich, personal email, September 23, 2019.

[73] Jung, *CW* 15 § 159, translation modified.

[74] Giegerich, personal email, September 23, 2019. By "absolute" Giegerich here means "absolved," in the Hegelian sense, from the difference between subjective and objective.

[75] Jung, *CW* 15 § 161, translation modified, Giegerich's italics.

not, as you point out, "a third person *a priori*,"[76] but the produced work, the result as the origin. [Again as Jung puts it:] "That which in the last analysis wills in him is not he, the human being as person, but the work of art."[77]

I want to cite a final passage from Jung that shows his having integrated what earlier had been so abhorrent to him—the anima's psychology-redefining suggestion that his work on his fantasies was art—into his later mature notion of psychology. At the end of his aforementioned essay on analytical psychology's relation to poetry, as also in a passage similar to this at the end of his essay on psychology and literature, Jung touches upon "the secret of great art, of its effect upon us."[78] This, he claims, is comparable to an individual dreaming such compensatory dreams as have been "activated by a deviation from the middle way."[79] The creative process of great art, in Jung's view, is likewise born of "the unconscious activation of an archetypal image, and in elaborating and shaping this image into a finished work."[80]—And "Therein lies the social significance of art: it is constantly at work educating the spirit of the age, conjuring up the forms in which the age is most lacking."[81] In Jung's time the spirit of the age was largely dominated by the positivism and materialistic prejudice of the so-called objective sciences, so much so, in fact, that the kinds of insight that Jung's "psychology *'with soul'*"[82] was concerned with were more or less foreclosed from the outset. The anima, however, in the story we heard about her from Jung, negated this prevailing position by offering (as Eve did the apple to Adam) her at first disconcerting, but ultimately soulful, assertion that what Jung regarded as psychology was in truth art. And the upshot of this was that aesthetics and the creative arts became, as it were, the speculative predicates of Jung's never abandoned, but rather, subtly deliteralized

[76] See p. 15-16 above.
[77] Jung, *CW* 15 § 158, translation modified. Cited here from Giegerich's personal email letter to me, 23 September 2019.
[78] *Ibid.* § 130.
[79] *Ibid.* § 160. The reference to "the middle way" is a reference to the Tao.
[80] *Ibid.* § 130.
[81] *Ibid.*
[82] Jung, *CW* 8 § 661, translation modified.

conception of psychology, which from that point on was continuously inspired by the animating insight, stated by Jung in his *Red Book*, that "my soul cannot be the object of my judgment and knowledge; much more are my judgment and knowledge the objects of my soul."[83]

Breaking the fourth wall

It will be recalled that at the beginning of this essay I cited the well-known sentence of Shakespeare's in which the great dramatist likens of the world to a theatre stage, men and women to the actors playing upon it. Extending the metaphor, I then applied it to those occasions of interpretive boldness in which a therapist speaks in such a way as to bring about the consulting-room equivalent of what in the theatre world is known as breaking the fourth wall.

But what does it mean, breaking the fourth wall? In theatre productions a drama's *mise-en-scène* is boxed in along three of its sides by a wall at the back of the stage and wings along each side, while its fourth side, technically known as the proscenium, is the assumed-to-exist, and in that sense, invisibly present wall that divides the stage set and its actors from the audience watching. It is when one of the actors, while remaining in character, suddenly exceeds the demure immediacy of his role in the drama by addressing statements to the audience, as if (breaking a leg to the power of two!) he now existed outside the play with them and they inside the play with him, that the fourth wall is broken.

It happens like this. In the drama that is being performed, the characters on the stage are at first fully immersed in their fictional sphere, as too are the audience members, watching in rapt attention. But then, breaking ranks as it were, one of the characters turns away from the others and speaks directly to the audience, subject to subject, I to I, while his companion characters seem for the duration of this to have been placed "on pause."—Or, the other way around, it may happen that an actor who is seated amongst the audience members, costumed as one of them, suddenly leaps up and addresses the players on the stage. Whichever way it is done, the effect of this obstreperous

---

[83] C. G. Jung, *The Red Book, Liber Novus*, Sonu Shamdasani, ed. (New York & London: W. W. Norton & Company, 2009), p. 232.

uprising is that the *participation mystique* with the *mise-en-scène*, which had until this point held sway, is both excited to a greater intensity and ironized at the same time, even as the difference between the fictional reality depicted in the drama and the literal reality of the audience outside (which had previously been no difference at all, those in attendance having quite forgotten about their extra-thespian lives) is established and collapsed, established and collapsed. All of which means, contrary to the glossary-like explanation I gave in the previous paragraph, that the fourth wall does not first exist, then to be broken, but only comes into being in the first place as the result of its being broken. And this, as we might call it, its negative provenance is provident as well of those moments in a play in which, speaking in the manner described, a character at once both sunders the afore-mentioned immediate unity (such that the players on the stage and the citizens in the audience are set off from one another) and mediates between them via a statement that overreaches this difference.

It is like what Jung was getting at when, in the context of alchemy, he spoke of "the separation and synthesis of psychic opposites."[84] Or, again, what Hegel was getting at when he described truth in terms of the identity of identity and difference. For when enjoined in the mutuality of the concept that at once both establishes and overreaches their difference (and which was presented *avant la lettre* by the character who broke the fourth wall!),[85] the players and the audience, the drama and the world outside, involutionally pass under and across into the unity, the identity, of their identity and difference, or as Hegel might also say, into the truth that is the whole and of which they in their separateness are but nuanced moments.

With these reflections in mind, we can return to our topic of the *vicarius animae*. Just as there are occasions in a play in which a character breaks the fourth wall (such that the audience's initial *participation mystique* with the *mise-en-scène* is broken and resumed, broken and resumed), so, too, are there occasions in psychotherapy in which the therapist addresses a statement, not to the patient directly as a fellow player within the transference or figure amongst

---

[84] The subtitle of Jung's *Mysterium Coniunctionis*—"An inquiry into the separation and synthesis of psychic opposites in Alchemy." *CW* 12.

[85] Present not necessarily in the content of what that character says, but via the mediating role he plays by addressing the audience.

others within a dream he has had, but on behalf of him as these to an audience, if I may still refer to it as that, consisting of what (glossing differences of theorization amongst a number of schools of thought) may variously be called language,[86] soul, symbolic order, third of the two, objective psyche, faith of the world, consciousness (in the sense of the transformations of its logical form) and the subject, amongst other names.[87]

It is what Jung was getting at when he said that the psyche is not in us, but rather, we that are in the psyche.[88] As if choreographed by this insight, the vicarius I-statement of the therapist, though leaven to be sure with what is known about the patient and his life situation on a psychic level, is addressed, not to him *per se*, but to the soul side of the psychological difference. And here as I state this, I am reminded in a flash of Jung's claim that "analytical psychology has burst the bonds which till then had bound it to the consulting-room of the doctor. It goes beyond itself [...]."[89]

What I am attempting to describe may be familiar to the reader from spirited moments of discourse within ordinary life. Two friends on a walk are in deep conversation when suddenly one of them stops in his tracks and "going on the record," as it were, addresses a high-spirited statement, not to his immediate interlocutor, but to the sky, the hills, and the environing surround. Similarly, turning away from the immediacy of the patient/therapist relation, the therapist addresses a speculative remark born of his having interiorized himself into the dream, symptom, or topic of

---

[86] Especially in the sense of Heidegger's insight that it is not we who speak, but language that speaks, and this, moreover, in a manner that brings everything that *is* out of concealment. As the philosopher puts it, "Words and language are not hulls into which we pack things for purposes of speech or correspondence. It is in the word and in language that things become and are things." Cited by Roberts Avens, *The New Gnosis, Heidegger, Hillman, and Angels* (Dallas: Spring Publications, 1984), p.49.

[87] Žižek's term is "ideology."

[88] "As I see it, the psyche is a world in which the ego is contained" (*CW* 13 § 75). "You rightly emphasize that man in my view is enclosed in *the* psyche (not in *his* psyche)." (14 May 1950, Letter to Joseph Goldbrunner, *Letters*, Vol. 1, p. 556). In our context, a finer point can be put on these statements. The psyche is not in us, the way psychic phenomena such as emotions and images are. Rather, we are in the psyche, i.e., *in its experience of itself.*

[89] Jung, *CW* 16 § 174.

concern they have been discussing, outward into the thoughtful upshot of these,[90] which is also to say, into the sphere of shared meanings, concepts, and background processes in which he and the patient culturally, narratively, and metaphysically inhere.

It is as if an offering is being made. Putting aside what the content discussed in the consulting-room has felt like or meant personally and experientially to the patient, a distillate of this (let us call it the evaporate result of the movement from substance to I-statement!) is being apostrophized by the therapist to consciousness-at-large or consciousness-as-such as to the true subject of feeling, meaning, and experiencing.[91] But here let us take stock. When earlier we discussed matters pertinent to this aspect of our theme, reference was made to "the coming to consciousness of the psychic process itself" (Jung) and to "the science of the experience of consciousness" (Hegel). These, it will be recalled, had in each case to do, not with what a person or a people experience on a psychic level, but with the experience that, auguring itself forward, the consciousness or concept they exist as has had of itself through them. Illustrative of this, let us again bear in mind, is the experience that the law may have of itself when, weighed against itself as against a feather, it is tested in one or another of the unique and infinitely varied human situations that from time to time require its highest courts. Along the same lines, to be recalled as well in our present context, is Jung's previously discussed reference to life putting a question to him (often by way of his patients) to which he must give his answer even as he was a question put to the world for it to answer.[92] And further to this characterization

---

[90] Compare here Jung's reference to the other "picture [that] looms up" when interpreting a dream. And compare this, in turn, to what we learned earlier (p. 85) from Hegel about the I. It is when a dream is no longer *imagined* as consisting of separate images vis-à-vis one another, but rather is *thought* by an I which produces itself in the first place as the negation and sublation of these, that what we are calling the consulting-room equivalent of "breaking the fourth wall" is achieved. C. G. Jung, *The Visions Seminars: Book One* (Zürich: Spring Publications, 1976), p. 8.

[91] Feeling in the higher sense intended here corresponds to Jung's description of it in his book on psychological types as a rational judgment of value. The meaning and experience referred to at the end of this sentence is predicated on this.

[92] The world's answer, presumably, would correspond to the changes in the way the world is logically structured and apperceived, which is also to say, to the various shapes that consciousness passes through in the course of its logical life. We could also see the world's answer as being reflected in changes in the patient's

from Jung of his psychological stance, an inspiring hint with respect to a therapist's directing vicarius I-statements beyond the consulting-room's equivalent of a theatre production's fourth wall may be gleaned from his comment, "I frequently have a feeling that [the dead] are standing directly behind us, waiting to hear what answer we will give to them, and what answer to destiny."[93] Adapting this to our purposes, we need only widen Jung's reference to the dead by taking this as a short-hand way of referring to psychology or "the soul" as "the historical presence of what is no longer a present reality."[94]

Generally speaking, we find in psychotherapy that a main difficulty that patients have has to do with their not having distinguished their present reality from some transference or other, be it personal or archetypal. The continuing presence of what is no longer a present reality is quixotically clung to, or if not clung to any longer then at least not yet explicitly departed from and allowed to be historical.[95] Therapeutically, the need is for an emancipation of the soul from anachronistic, obdurately substantiated forms of itself to the form of itself as I,[96] which, as we learned from Hegel, "is the universal, in which abstraction is made from everything particular, but in which at the same time everything is present, though veiled."[97] Functioning on behalf of the patient as the mediator of "thinking itself,"[98] the therapist distills an I-statement from out of the session's or soul situation's *mise-en-scène*, the utterance of which, like the ring of truth, carries beyond the soundproof walls of the consulting room, not literally, of course, to passersby outside, but logically, psychologically, to the sphere of shared values and meanings,

---

dreamscapes following his having owned up to something that he had not acknowledged before. In response to such learning and insight, the kaleidoscope shifts, as it were, and a new landscape appears. Whitman writes: "Have you reckoned the landscape took substance and form that it might be painted in a picture [by you]?" *Leaves of Grass*, p. 91, line 82.

[93] Jung, *MDR*, p. 308.

[94] Giegerich, *CEP* IV, p. 474, fn. 16.

[95] For a thoroughgoing analysis of neurosis as the soul's clinging to former statuses of itself which are no longer true, see Wolfgang Giegerich, *Neurosis: The Logic of a Metaphysical Illness* (New Orleans: Spring Journal Books, 2013).

[96] On the topic of the soul's emancipation of itself from itself see: Wolfgang Giegerich, *What is Soul?* pp. 317-335.

[97] Hegel (as per the *Zusätze*): *EL* § 24, p. 57.

[98] *Ibid.*

conceptions and ideals that, in a manner comparable to that of a Möbius strip, have just as much thrown their voices into the discourse of the patient and therapist, finding thereby, through their being questioned and differentiated from in the course of what had seemed to be therapeutic work on an exclusively personal level, remedy in what Hegel called the moments of the particular and the singular for a universality that would otherwise have been too anachronistic, bloodless, and abstract.

It is what Jung was getting at with that claim of his about analytical psychology having burst the bonds of the consulting room. What Jung had in mind when he stated this was a widening of the scope of psychotherapy beyond its immediate clinical purpose, the better to fulfill that purpose. No longer was therapy to be understood exclusively as method of treatment, but as a method of "self-education and self-perfection"[99] as well.

Now it is important to grasp that with these terms Jung was referring to something completely different from the "psycho-education" that in our times has largely displaced the studious interest that psychotherapy had traditionally taken in the individual, replacing this with what might be described as a life-style magazine mentality wherein patients are persuaded to identify with one or another of the pathologies and potentialities that have been offered to them by the marketplace that psychology has increasingly become. As referenced by him, self-education and self-perfection had rather to do with the enlargement of consciousness via a close examination and integration of the arrows and slings, contradictions and compensations, that arise when an individual is thrown back upon himself in an individuality-activating way by the vicissitudes of life, on the one hand, and the wrangles of the transference, on the other. [100] They were not, for him, commodities sold to us from outside the way that they are today.

But here we are. In our times amongst patients who come garbed from the outset in the identifications mentioned. It is like when people go to the movies dressed in the period costumes of the

---

[99] Jung, *CW* 16 § 174.

[100] We have already heard from Jung that "in a way nothing ever happens to you which you are not. The life you live is your life. All your experiences are yourself—that is exactly what you are." For the full quotation, see p. 85 above.

characters in the film being shown. Speaking in acronyms picked up from internet searches, it frequently happens that we are told by a new patient in the opening minutes of an initial session that he or she *has* "BPD," "NPD," "OCD," or something of the sort and are asked in the same breath if we *do* "CBT," DBT, NLP, etc. Or it is some kind of enjoyment or performance-enhancement they are shopping for—communication skills, self-esteem, mindfulness, to name only these. Putting all this in terms of our theatre analogy, we can say that dressed in such brand name clothes, the informed consumers that our patients have of late become are just as much seated outside their therapy in the audience as they are in their therapy, players upon its stage.—Indeed, it is quite as if the proscenium or fourth wall, in the undialectical, glossary definition sense of that term, runs through them, or better, through psychology dividing it from itself, hence the need for the therapist to break through this divide.—Or has it already been broken, already collapsed, by a television psychologist, perhaps? But this in a way that leaves the patient in his singularity and uniqueness out of account, neither in nor out, here nor there?

What then is the real "self-education and self-perfection"? Carried forward in the spirit intended by Jung,[101] the meaning of

---

[101] With regards to the *letter* of Jung's statement, the last words of what I quoted of this— "It goes beyond itself"—continue with the words: "to fill the hiatus that has hitherto put Western civilization at a psychic disadvantage as compared to the civilizations of the East. We Westerners knew only how to tame and subdue the psyche; we knew nothing about its methodological functions" (*CW* 16 § 174). I would advise that this reference of Jung's to the wisdom traditions of the East as being compensatory to the one-sided development of the West (in another place he writes that our "growing familiarity with the spirit of the East should be taken merely as a sign that we are beginning to relate to the alien elements within ourselves"—*CW* 13 § 72.) needs to be read in terms of the description of his style of psychotherapy, in its difference from the therapies of Freud and Adler, which is to be found Chapters IV-VIII of his "On the Psychology of the Unconscious" (*CW* 7 § 56-201). The emphasis on the problem of the attitude type and on the problem of the opposites and their integration discussed in those chapters corresponds to what Jung had in mind when he wrote in the line above those I quoted of "plac[ing] all the implements of the psychotherapeutic art [...] at the service of our self-education and self-perfection [...]" (*CW* 16 § 174). This, surely, is what Jung meant when he claimed that psychotherapy had surpassed itself as a merely clinical enterprise to "serve the common weal" (*CW* 16 § 174).

these terms has to do with the continuous imparting of the experience to which psychology owes it provenance beyond the bounds of the consulting room. This experience, as we know, is its experience of itself—we could also say, its experience of itself as the insightful I-statement that comes to mind as the speculative result of the melting down of the abstract universals that are ambient in the atmosphere beyond its immediate confines in the solvent of the individual patient and his singular predicament.[102] For, indeed, as Jung goes on to put it a few sentences down from the statements cited, "as soon as psychotherapy takes the doctor himself for its subject, it transcends its medical origins and ceases to be merely a method for treating the sick. It now treats the healthy or such as has a moral right to psychic health, whose sickness is at most the suffering that torments us all."[103]

Nota bene, the doctor himself! Or what in these pages we have called the therapist as *vicarius animae*. Psychology itself as bodied-forth by the psychotherapist within the auspices of the patient's *mise-en-scène*.

Above I used a variety of terms to refer to the soul-side of the psychological difference—consciousness-at-large, symbolic order, the subject, etc. In that play called Psychotherapy, Transference, or

---

[102] Compare here Jung's statement, "We always find in the patient a conflict which at a certain point is connected with the great problems of society. Hence, when the analysis is pushed to this point, the apparently individual conflict of the patient is revealed as a universal conflict of his environment and epoch. Neurosis is thus nothing less that an individual attempt, however unsuccessful, to solve a universal problem; indeed it cannot be otherwise, for a general problem, a 'question,' is not an *ens per se*, but exists only in the hearts of individuals" (*CW* 7 § 438. See also *CW* 7 § 18). Along the same lines, on another occasion Jung opined that there are not a few neurotics "who do not require any reminders of their social duties and obligations, but are born and destined rather to be bearers of new cultural ideals" (*CW* 4 § 658). Though highly apt in our context, the view that Jung asserts in these passages has been strongly contradicted by Giegerich (*What is Soul?* pp. 330-331). Resolving this dispute, I would offer that the observations of Jung are valid if the emphasis is shifted from the neurosis and the neurotic patient to the therapist as *vicarius animae* giving to the patient's soul-situation the form of psychology, the form of the I, by inwardizing it into itself. And further to this, I would recall from decades ago in our literature, David L. Miller's emphasis upon "the therapy of ideas" and James Hillman's emphasis upon "the '*infirmitas*' of the archetype." All of these are attempts to depart from personalistic psychology and to deal with the objective dimension of subjectivity.

[103] Jung, *CW* 16 § 174.

Consulting Room, it is the therapist, cast in the role of mediator of this, that from time to time turns away from the character that is being played by the patient to present on his behalf the vocal upshot of the unity of the unity and difference of what would otherwise stand divided in accordance with the ordinarily prevailing subject here/object there, players here/attending public there difference of consciousness, on the one hand, or naively and immediately united via "the suggestive power of fantasy images,"[104] on the other. This is not to say that he knows in advance that the utterance he is venturing will express the logic that pervades both sides of this divide. The therapist doesn't know this at all, except, perhaps, after the fact when it seems to have happened.[105] For he is always "*only* that!*,*" only a psychotherapist, or rather (at once both less than that and more), only the unity of the unity and difference of the person he is and his professional role, on the one hand, the patient and his situation, on the other.

Now, of course, the words I just quoted in the previous sentence are from Jung's well-known statement, "The greatest limitation for man is the 'self'; it is manifested in the experience: 'I am *only* that!'" In Jung's view, "Only consciousness of our narrow confinement in the self forms the link to the unconscious," or as he also puts it, the link to "the infinite."[106] But what does it mean in our context, "I am *only* that!"? The answer becomes apparent when these words are read as a speculative sentence.[107] It will be recalled that such a reading requires that the predicate be read, not merely as a quality of the subject, but as being essential, that is, as the subject a second time, itself more acutely defined. To read our statement from Jung in this manner is to realise that it is not that I, in addition to being

---

[104] Jung's reference to "the suggestive power of primordial images," *CW* 7 § 269.

[105] It remains to be seen if the statement made by the therapist is merely an imitative statement mirroring of the patient on a psychic and/or egoic level, or if it is truly a speculative one on the psychological level. See pp. 26-27 above for a discussion of this distinction.

[106] Jung, *MDR*, p. 325.

[107] For a related treatment of this topic, focusing on these same words of Jung, see my "Inwardizing an underlined sentence into itself: Some reflections on being '*only* that!', in Jennifer Sandoval & John Knapp, eds., *Psychology as the Discipline of Interiority: The Psychological Difference in the Work of Wolfgang Giegerich* (London & New York: Routledge, 2017), pp. 66-81.

what I positively already am, have the modesty or diminutiveness of being "*only* that" as my additional quality. Rather, "only thatness" is what, in the negativity of its provenance, the I as which I am *is*. The I, or as this may also be called, the "*only* that," is negative to whatever else there may be, which is also to say, the result of, or return from, the otherness of all that it is not.—And with this we are brought back yet again to Hegel's account of the I as "the universal, in which abstraction is made from everything particular, but in which at the same time everything is present, though veiled."[108] I should only want to add that the same goes for psychology. It, too, is both abstraction from, and sublated expression of, all that it is not. It, too, an I that is "*only* that!" Indeed, as Jung put it, "Psychology is neither biology nor physiology nor any other science than just the knowledge of the soul."[109]

So dense have been the reflections and elaborations of the last few paragraphs that it may seem that we are now a far cry from the analogy I drew between the therapist's vicarius I-statement and a character in a play's breaking of the fourth wall. To recover our sense of this, it needs only to be grasped that the *tertium comparationis* of these is an I that, having produced itself via its having abstracted itself from everything particular,[110] while at the same time containing all that it has abstracted itself from under sublation in what Hegel called its night,[111] is in Jung's sense "*only* that!" Just as we all, as Shakespeare put it, fret our hour upon the stage of life, now as this character, now as that, so the I, as the unity of the unity and difference of all that it is not, does too. In a play as the statement of an actor that breaks the fourth wall. In psychotherapy via the vicarius I-statement of the therapist that "burst[s] the bonds which till then had bound it to the consulting room."[112]

---

[108] Hegel (as per the *Zusätze*), *EL*, § 24, p. 57.

[109] Writes Jung in the German edition of his collected works, "Psychologie is aber weder Biologie noch Physiologie noch irgendine andere Wissenshaft als eben das Wissen um die Seele." *GW* 9i § 63.

[110] Abstraction from everything is what the I *is*. It does not first exist and then abstract itself.

[111] See p. 44 above.

[112] Jung, *CW* 16 § 174. For further insight into the subtleties involved in breaking out of the consulting-room mentality, see Giegerich's critique of

Speculative personality and the name-giving power of the I

My aim in this final section is to end on an inspiring note by reflecting our topic in a statement of Hegel's about the personality and a statement of Jung's about the I. Eminently suited for this purpose, what is remarkable about these passages is their near hierophantic character. There is something majestic enunciating itself in these passages, and this I take as an indication of voice being given in them to the soul-side of the psychological difference. Which in our psychotherapeutic context is what vicarius I-statements are about as well.

But here now, hasn't psychology long given up on the soul, reduced it to the personality, explained it away? As usually conceived of in academic and clinical psychology, personality belongs exclusively to the psychic-side, the ego-side, of what for them (being unmindful of the psychological difference) is no difference at all. It is made up of traits that are measurable and qualities that can be predicated of the person. Of instincts and the vicissitudes of these, driving him in the manner of the tail that wagged the dog. And the ego, too, is conceived as something thing-like and positively existing, even Jung conceiving of it as a complex amongst others. How then soul? How then, given this materialistic prejudice, is subjectivity in the eminent sense that we still have in mind when we resort to that bygone term, to assert itself in the context of our work with patients?

With this our interest in the interpretive mode of the vicarius I-statement in mind, let us turn to our first passage. Writing with respect to personhood, Hegel declares:

> Man's chief glory is to be a person, and yet in spite of that the bare abstraction, "person" is somewhat contemptuous in its very expression. "Person" is essentially different from "subject," since "subject" is only the possibility of personality; every living thing of any sort is a subject. A person, then, is a subject aware of his subjectivity, since in personality it is of myself alone that I am

---

Hillman's undialectical attempt to overcome personalistic psychology via a literal shift away from individual analysis in favour of working with large groups and giving public lectures, etc. Giegerich, *The Soul's Logical Life*, pp. 191-201.

aware. A person is a unit of freedom aware of its sheer independence. As *this* person, I know myself to be free in myself. I can abstract from everything, since nothing confronts me save pure personality, and yet as *this* person I am something wholly determinate, e.g., I am of a certain age, a certain stature, I occupy this space, and so on through whatever details you like. This personality is at once the sublime and the trivial. It implies this unity of the infinite with the purely finite, of the wholly limitless with determinate limitation. It is the sublimity of personality that is able to sustain this contradiction, a contradiction which nothing merely natural contains or could endure.[113]

It is notable that with the contrast drawn by Hegel in the first sentence of this passage that what we call the psychological difference is readily established. By Hegel's lights, there is a higher sense of being a person and a lower one. In its highest determination, being a person is the human subject's greatest glory, the fulfillment of its concept, as it were. But it is also the case that when taken too abstractly "person" designates a much more meager determination of subjectivity, as for example when we qualify an opinion with the caveat that it is "*only* personal." Being only personal, in this derogatory sense, means to be utterly contingent and lacking universality.[114] What's more, it can also mean that when an experience is being spoken of, what is said by the person to have happened is presented by him or her in an unreflected manner, as a mere content of consciousness, while the possibly form-changing, logic-shifting experience that consciousness has at the same time had of itself is being left out of account. And such may be the case with all manner of comments and observations. These, too, may be

---

[113] G. W. F. Hegel, *Hegel's Philosophy of Right*, T. M. Knox, trans. (London, Oxford, New York: Oxford University Press, 1976), p. 235. Passage is from the "Additions" appendix. Such additions are based on notes and transcriptions taken by attendees of Hegel's lectures on the topic discussed.

[114] For the sake of the subtly of the matter, I should also mention the not so different other side of this coin wherein a person is subject to an inflationary excess of universality, as when, for example, a concept or idea goes to his head. Significantly, in our context, this goes for the *concept*, "Person," as well, which, often by way of its aliases, Freedom and Rights, is bandied about in the matter of an abstract universal, that is, without reference to the particulars that make the person who has gotten carried away to be *this* person, in *this* life, with *these* challenges and responsibilities.

trotted out by an I that cannot see past the nose on its own face, "the I that is a We and the We that is an I" be damned. True personality, by contrast, designates a determination of the subject that holds the universal and the contingent together in itself (or better, produces the universal in the first place out of its holding all manner of immediate contingencies and surrounding contextual factors together in what becomes thereby their mutually mediating nullity) and this, moreover, as I should additionally like to add, in a manner productive of the naming of things and the voicing of truths. Personhood, it follows, is the upshot, the precipitate result, of the negations which as personality it self-productively negates in its turn. Just as we repeatedly heard from Hegel in the last few sections about the I being the sublatedness of all that it is not, so in this passage is personhood and personality similarly described. As a person "I can abstract from everything [...] and yet as *this* person I am something wholly determinate." And it is from this, as I like to call it, the *coniunctio* of our being as free as Adam, on the one hand, and as limited as Eve on the other, that our powers to know things and to name them stems. "Just as Adam said to Eve: 'Thou art flesh of my flesh and bone of my bone', so mind says: 'This is mind of my mind and its foreign character has disappeared.'[115] In our context as well, knowing and naming is a function of investing one's freedom as an I into the finitude of whatever the phenomena may be that has captured one's interest,[116] and this in such a way that the various moments of its internal dialectic speculatively come home to themselves in the unity of the unity and difference of their being known from within by me—consummating my personhood and actualizing my personality thereby.

Now it is important to emphasize that the phrase, "abstract[ing] from everything," does not only mean abstracting from what, owing to the ordinarily prevailing subject-object distinction, appears to be other and external.[117] It refers as well to a determination of subjectivity that is born of abstraction having been made from the

---

[115] Hegel, *Hegel's Philosophy of Right*, p. 226. The passage is from the Additions appendix. For a fuller treatment of this passage, see pp. 19-20 above.

[116] In a dream, a symptom, or life situation—whatever the subject matter of the moment may be.

[117] I say "appears" here because, as we also know from both Hegel and Jung, what I experience is always mine.

psychic contents of the personality as well, that is, from all the complexes, traits, and biographical details that make up the person and his personality in the positive sense of these as they are studied by academic and clinical psychology. And it is owing to this, let us call it the determinately-negating, abstracting proclivity of the soul as I, that the therapist can speak in the first person vicarius, which is also to say, on the patient's behalf as that "sublimity of personality," actualized in the form of insights and I-statements, that has, or is as, the speculative strength to sustain the contradiction of having been produced via abstraction from everything, on the one hand, while being wholly bound by all manner of conditioning factors (i.e., the concerns of the patient, psychic and circumstantial), on the other.

It has to be both, what the therapist says, universal and particular at the same time. Only the patient can report on or speak from the psychic side of the psychological difference. Only he can say what he thinks and feels about this, that, or the other thing (though the therapist, of course, may assist him in this, sometimes by making empathic comments, at other times by way of imitative ones).[118] For he alone is "*this* person." [119] Statements made on a patient's behalf from the soul-side of the psychological difference, by contrast, have the character of holding the concept "Person" in its universality and the facts and details associated with *this* particular person together in a speculative remark.[120] And the same goes for whatever the particulars of a situation may be. It is their adequation to their concepts, whatever these may be, that the vicarius I-statements of the talking cure are about. Never mind that in their particularity the universals that are needing to be named or re-named may first appear

---

[118] As was discussed on pp. 24-25 in Part One above.

[119] I said that only the patient can report on or speak from the psychic side of the psychological difference. But if we are more strict in our assessment, we have to realize that while no one can do this for him, it is also the case that not even he can truly do so, this because, as Hegel has pointed out in that section of the *Phenomenology* in which he critiques sense-certainty, what seems to be immediate experience—in our context here, immediate psychic experience—is already mediated by the universals of language. And these are often not adequate to what they describe, express, give words to, and name. Which is why talk therapy in the speculative sense of this that I propose here is needed. To bring about a truer degree of adequation between the particular and the universal, the thing and its concept, the psychic and the psychological.

[120] For a discussion of Hegel's "speculative remark" see pp. 71-72 above.

as limiting symptoms. Nothing falls outside the concept, outside the soul. Least of all those limiting moments of particularity and finitude that agitate its dialectic and make it real. For again, as we learned earlier from Hegel, "the I, as knowing or thinking in general, is limited but knows about the limit, and in this very knowledge the limit is only a limit, only something negative outside us, and I am beyond it."[121] So, too, the personality in the higher sense discussed by Hegel. It, too, is limited, but knowingly so, and to that extent released; subjective, and yet aware of this, and to that extent free.

With the above reflections in mind, and for the sake of the further inspiration it may provide to the psychotherapist in his role of *vicarius animae*, let us now turn to a passage from Jung in which consciousness, the I, and the naming of what is are again brought together in a majestic way:

> All the worlds that have ever existed before man were physically *there*. But they were a nameless happening, not a definite actuality, for there did not yet exist that minimal concentration of the psychic factor, which was also present, to speak the word that outweighed the whole of Creation: That is the world, and this is I! That was the first morning of the world, the first sunrise after the primal darkness, when the inchoately conscious complex, the ego, the son of the darkness, knowingly sundered subject and object, and thus precipitated the world and itself into definite existence, giving it and itself a voice and a name.[122]

The first thing to be noted in this marvelous text is the tribute that is paid in it to the soul side of the psychological difference. The "psychic factor," without which the world would be neither known nor named, is discussed by Jung, not in the measly sense in which we usually speak of it in contrast to the psychological, but in its cosmogonic significance. And the same goes for the ego and the I. Given out as synonyms, these, too, are referred to in their largest and most tremendous sense, not merely as parts of the personality or contents of some greater reality, but as the world-outweighing,

---

[121] G.W. F. Hegel, *Lectures on the Philosophy of Religion, One-Volume Edition. The Lectures of 1827*, Peter C. Hodgson, ed., R. R. Brown, P. C. Hodgson, and J. M. Stewart, trans. (Berkeley, Los Angeles, London: University of California Press, 1988), p. 173.

[122] Jung, *CW* 14 § 129.

ontology-upending, consciousness-yielding, mere being-sublating, (I would also add) will-galvanizing reflection of any-and-all worlds co-equally into themselves as the voicing and the naming of what *is*.

Now, for our purposes as therapists the most interpretation-emboldening lines in this text are those having to do with the psychic factor's "speak[ing] the word that outweighed the whole of Creation." The language here is positively biblical, or rather, in our sense negatively so. In John's gospel we read the great words: "In the beginning there was the Word."[123] In Jung's we read: "That is the world, and this is I!"[124] The reader will be reminded by this statement of our earlier discussion of the exuberant cry that Jung gives out in the part of his memoirs in which he recalls his having gazed out over the great rivers of migrating animal herds while on safari in East Africa: "Man, I, in an invisible act of creation put the stamp of perfection on the world by giving it objective existence."[125] Of course, in the text of Jung's we are now discussing, Jung is only referring, great as this already is, to the "minimal concentration of the psychic factor" that our earliest forebearers were able to muster. Significantly, this he extolls as already the I. How much more so, now, these many aeons later, the power of subjectivity, the weightiness and acuity of the I! How much greater, today, the concentration of the psychic factor! Again, to fully appreciate this, we have to think the provenance of this speculatively. It is not just that *Homo sapiens sapiens* had, in addition to their biological being, a glimmer of consciousness as their additional property. Nor was this glimmer, for all the aptness of its being compared to the first sunrise (in Jung's words, to "the first morning of the world"), something additional coming from outside in the way the light of the actual sun does. Rather, the glimmer that made early man to be Man in the first place came from within his exposure to existence (or better, from the exposure of Existence to

---

[123] *John* 1:1.

[124] *That* and *this*, *world* and *I*, these "are different, but the same," even as for Parmenides, the same things exist for thinking as for being.

[125] Jung, *MDR*, p. 255.

itself through him[126]), even as it subsequently continued to provide for and shine forth from his being-in-the-world.

After this excursus let us return to our principal theme. Speaking on our behalf, even as we on occasion speak as and on behalf of our patients, the great psychologist vicariusly declares: "That is the world, and this is I." What Jung gives us here is the form of truth. Not epistemological truth, but soul truth. Truth in the sense of "the world of life as it really happens to be plus the determined presence of man, his entrance into, and logical self-exposure to life."[127] As analytic psychotherapists we need an analytical stance that is as deep, vast, and overarching as is the account given by Jung of the speculative identity of what he calls that world and this I. In common with the need of our patients to see their dilemmas and life-situations from within, we need a vision of the psychological, or better, a *conception* of this, wherein, pulled up by its own bootstraps, the I stands resoundingly in the centre of its varied and mysterious apperceived landscapes. How else take seriously Jung's insight about our having as psychologists no Archimedean vantage point outside the psyche, outside the world, to view it from objectively?[128] How else soul truth but for the inwardization of whatever is of compelling concern Archimedeanlessly into itself? It is what Jung was getting at when in a related context he characterized the psyche as "the world's pivot."[129] Negative to what is, and yet, the sublatedness at the same time of all that it is not, the psyche as subjectivity, the soul as I, is (in Jung's phrase again) "the word that outweighed the whole of Creation," imparting itself in the form of the names by which the world is known.—"That is the world, and this is I," indeed!

---

[126] For a discussion of the origins of consciousness in the exposure of existence to itself via the practice of ritual sacrifice in the ancient world see W. Giegerich, "Killings," in his *CEP* III, pp. 189-265.

[127] Giegerich, *The Soul's Logical Life*, p. 225. Note the word "plus" in this sentence. Truth is both the world *and* one's exposure to this, in other words, the logic that pervades both.

[128] Jung, *CW* 8 § 421, § 429.

[129] Writes Jung, "The psyche is the world's pivot: not only is it the one great condition for the existence of the world at all, it is also an intervention in the existing natural order, and no one can say with certainty where this intervention will finally end." *CW* 8 § 423.

Is this what we are here for, writes Rilke in his *Duino Elegies,* to say House, Bridge, Fountain, Tower, Jug, etc.? Is this what we are here for, to behold and to name what would otherwise be unknown, untrue? It is helpful to realize that Personality in the speculative sense I am attempting to convey (and we can include in this its heart of hearts the I) is always already and ever again the result to begin with of the distinction-making, name-originating dialectical movement adumbrated by Hegel in his *Encyclopaedia Logic.* For just as "Being" (the first term of the great sequence of terms discussed in that book[130]) notionally runs afoul of itself as being indistinguishable from "Nothing," but this in such a way that its contravention of its concept finds resolution in the notion of "Becoming," and just as, Geist of its own history, it happens again and again that each subsequent term or name, upon finding its limiting contradiction, goes under and across via the negation-negating knowledge of its limitedness to the next, so in our text from Hegel we find that "subject" passes over into its untruth, this via the realization that everything living is a subject.—And it is with this, the realization that in speaking of subject or of being a subject we are not saying what we mean (the concept being inadequate to is content) that we get "Person," even as via a similar dialectic the spurious abstractness of this concept is negated and sublated by the mediating particularity of *this* person to Personality.[131]

Now, it might be objected, here at the end of this essay, that the passages I have quoted from Hegel and Jung are more inspirational than practical. Ours is an age of methods and techniques. Practicing

---

[130] Hegel, *EL* § 88, p. 141.

[131] We have to realize that what we, drawing upon an insight from Hegel, have throughout this essay been calling the movement from substance to subject, is in our psychotherapeutic context the further moment from substance known as subject to person and personality. Person is both a concept, a universal, and as *this* person, something existing and particular. Personality, it follows, is the sublatedness of the two, manifesting and providing for our each being who we are via the concrete universality of the I. As universal, personality is there from the beginning (as Jung says of the I in our passage from him). Clearly, this is not personality in the personalistic sense of empirical psychology, but Personality in the sense Hegel has in mind when he identifies God to have personality character. And this, as it might also be called, absolute subjectivity, is the imparting of Personality to all that there is to be known via the names that it gives.

therapists want to know how to set about their business. Much like their patients, they want to know what they should do. To this I reply that the inspiration/practicality difference is a version of the psychological difference, and that it is from this, and especially from its soul-side, that the therapist, at least in those moments when he functions as *vicarius animae*, must take his marching orders.

What I am insisting upon here is pretty much the same as the point Jung makes in that supervisory admonishment of his we discussed in Part One of this essay:

> The analyst must give credit to his own interpretation. He must have courage, he must help; [otherwise] it is as if a man is bleeding to death and you *ponder!*[132] [...] It must be the best you can do. No cheating, no flippancy or routine; then the devil is after you. You must be honest about whether it is really the best you can do. If it is the best before God that you can do, then you can count on things going the right way. But it may be the wrong way. We go through difficult things; that is fate.[133]

To some, I am sure, this passage may come across as a counsel of recklessness. Especially so when contrasted with the meticulous technical recommendations that have accrued over the course of the long history of psychoanalytic psychotherapy. It is important to realize, however, that it is no hapless "flying by the seat of one's pants" that Jung is encouraging. While it is true that he offers no technique as such, there is a criterion, and a lofty one at that. Making passionate appeal to what we have called the vertical dimension, Jung insists that the interpretations ventured by the therapist must be the best he can do before God! —Or as we would prefer, adapting this

---

[132] While Jung, in keeping with his strong sense of the reality of the psyche, encouraged bold interpretive efforts to help patients, he also cautioned against the *furor sanandi*. He wrote: "[...] in psychology it is important that the doctor should not strive to heal at all costs. One has to be exceedingly careful not to impose one's own will and conviction on the patient. We have to give him a certain amount of freedom. You can't wrest people away from their own fate, just as in medicine you cannot cure a patient if nature means him to die. [...] You cannot save certain people from committing terrible nonsense because it is in their grain. Jung, *CW* 18 § 291.

[133] C. G. Jung, *C. G. Jung Speaking: Interviews and Encounters*, William McGuire and R. F. C. Hull, eds. (Princeton, N.J.: Princeton University Press, 1977), p. 360.

to our times, *post mortem Dei*, the best he can do before that successor notion of soul in the form of God, the soul as I.

But what about the patient, something incorrigible in us still asks? In a text in which he reflects the psychological difference in terms of a distinction drawn by those of the alchemists who, as he put it, "abhorred all vulgar substances and replaced them by 'symbolic' ones which allowed the nature of the archetype to glimmer through," Jung crucially adds:

> This does not mean that the adept ceased to work in the laboratory, only that he kept an eye on the symbolic aspect of his transmutations. This corresponds exactly to the situation in the modern psychology of the unconscious: while personal problems are not overlooked (the patient himself takes very good care of that!), the analyst keeps an eye on their symbolic aspects, for healing comes only from what leads the patient beyond himself and beyond his entanglement in the ego.[134]

A nice description, this, of the speculative acuity of the analytic psychotherapist. Elsewhere on the same page, Jung again insightfully observes: "modern man, caught in the toils of egohood, uses his personal psychological problems as a *façon de parler*."[135] Generalized into the form of a heuristic adage, the psychological difference is once again observed. Whereas in former times there had been "a religious formula for everything psychic—and one that is far more beautiful and comprehensive than immediate experience,"[136] in our post-religious, post-metaphysical times, the sunken equivalent of this, the soul's speaking about itself, tends to occur in the secularized dialect of personal psychological problems. In keeping with this, the challenge for the therapist is to speak in such a way as to give words and names to the values and concepts that the patient's problems and life-situation mutely imply.[137] These words and names, it is important

---

[134] Jung, *CW* 13 § 397.

[135] Jung, *CW* 13 § 396.

[136] Jung, *CW* 9i, § 11.

[137] Making much the same point, Jung elsewhere states: "The irrational factors that manifest themselves indirectly as 'incest complexes' and 'infantile fantasies,' etc. are susceptible of a quite different interpretation. They are psychic forces which other ages and other cultures have viewed in a different light. To experience this other side one should have the courage, for once, not to rationalize the

to emphasize, must come from a speculative reading of patient's soul-situation, and not from the psychological literature. Moreover, this reading, as I am calling it, must be performed by the therapist as an I that, while enjoying the freedom of its being negative to everything that there is, is at the same time totally limited by the matter at hand, that is, by the patient as the person he happens to be, the particulars of his life-situation, the specifics of his dreams.[138] For, as Hegel puts it in a line that transposes nicely into our context, "What is looked for here is the effort to give up this freedom [the negative freedom that constitutes the I—G.M.], and, instead of being the arbitrary moving principle of the content, to sink this freedom in the content, letting it move spontaneously of its own nature, by the self as its own self, and then to contemplate this movement."[139]

Above I paraphrased the line of Rilke's in which he wonders vicariously, on behalf of us all, if in ultimate regards our being here is for the sake of giving voice to the names of all that there is in the

---

statements of the unconscious but to take them seriously" (Jung to Anonymous, 5 February 1934, his *Letters*, vol. 1, pp. 142-143).

[138] The I's being negative to what is does not mean that it provides a view from nowhere or from some abstractly posited outside. We should think of it, rather, as a negative inwardness, Archimedeanless and abysmal. Rilke speaks in one of his *Sonnets to Orpheus* of loving in the swing of a figure nothing so much as the point of inflection (part two, sonnet 12). Likewise, in a sense exactly opposite to the idea of an Archimedean point, the I is the absolutely imbedded inflection point wherein ontology gives way to logic, Being to the terms of First Philosophy that determine themselves out of it, and the Being of each thing to its concept, its essence, its name. And the same goes for cognition, selfhood and personality. Part and parcel of each other, they, too, being logically negative, should not be conceived of as existing before the thoughts they have and the names they give. Rather, they should only be conceived of speculatively, performatively, as again and again the definitional and re-definitional somersaulting headlong plunge of what is into itself. Which is also to say, as inflection points, pivot points. Now with these reflections in mind we can return to psychotherapy. It is when a patient has fallen into a condition of having ceased to impart himself as a name-giving power that he complains of being abject in his mood, depersonalized, or stuck. And so it is, in response to this, that therapy takes on the philosophical character of being a therapy, not of the person in the personalistic sense (though this it may also be), but in a manner comparable to the conversations that Socrates held with his interlocutors, of the ideas that he and we exist as.

[139] Hegel, *PhS*, § 58, p. 36. Cf, "When I think, I give up my subjective particularity, sink myself in the matter, let thought follow its own course; and I think badly whenever I add something of my own." Hegel (as per the *Zusätze*), *EL* § 24, p. 58.

world to behold. How similar, this, to the passages from Hegel and Jung that we have been discussing! In closing, I only want to take this purpose that the poet has so evocatively posited to heart for our theme. This, as we have been discussing in such varied ways throughout the entirety of this essay, has to do with occasions in psychotherapy in which a therapist, having steeped himself in the soul-situation of the patient, ventures a comment on the latter's behalf in the form of an I-statement. Such comments and interpretations, I emphasized, have phenomenon character. Far from being intended by the therapist in the manner of a technique which he would apply from without, they are just statements that in inspired moments he is moved to say. At the same time, however, negating this eschewing of technique, I then went on to provide numerous reflections and analogies for the purpose of fostering in the therapist the speculative wherewithal to function on such occasions as *vicarius animae.* And now, here again, after what we have discussed in this section with respect to Personality and the I, we can put a finer point on the matter. In their most acute sense, vicarius I-statements have to do with speaking on behalf of the patient, not as a mere subject with such and such a psychology,[140] but as subject in the eminent sense, that is, as a "Person" who, in accordance with that concept in its highest sense, is at once both "a unit of freedom aware of its sheer independence" and as *"this* person" limited by all manner of inner facts and outer circumstances.—And the upshot of this "sustaining," as Hegel called it, of the contradictory unity of the "wholly limitless with determinate limitation" is Personality in its highest-determination as "the name-giving power," or as this has also been called, the I as "thinking itself.[141] For it is not merely on behalf of the patient as a mere subject amongst other subjects that the therapist makes I-statements. Rather, it is on behalf of the patient as Personality, the patient as I.

In the final analysis it vapors up and distills down to this. Weighing in as that I which is nothing else than the sublated result of its having abstracted from everything,[142] the *particular* therapist

---

[140] For a discussion of the fallacy of psychology as the study of people's psychologies see W. Giegerich, *The Soul's Logical Life,* pp. 123- 130.

[141] Hegel (as per the *Zusätze*), EL § 24, p. 57.

[142] This is achieved, in part, by tapping into the "I that is a We and the We that is an I" (Hegel) which is always already available to us all.

that despite this negation of myself I nevertheless still am, sink *my* Freedom, *my* Personality, *my* I, not merely into the limitations of my patient and his life-situation in their positivity (though this, to be sure, I may initially do), but speculatively, prospectively, into the "as if" of his implicitly having already done the same with respect to the world that, but for his hemming and hawing, it is *his* calling to name and to know.[143] We both have the same task, my patient and I: to know the truth as substance and subject, or again, to name what is via the I. Which is why, so long as he still needs me to, I will say on behalf of the poet in him, what he if he were able would say for the world: "That is the world, and this is I,"—House, Bridge, Fountain, Tower, Jug and so on ….

---

[143] In his Jena lecture, Hegel speaks of language as "the name-giving power." By this I take him to mean that language, via its mouthpiece, the soul as I, imparts itself and returns into itself in such a way that it knows, names, and expresses itself as the being of its object, the meaning of the thing, in other words, as the self-character of these. In the example of this that Hegel provides, it is shown that it is only in the sublatedness of a name that predicates which are merely descriptive of a thing come together to disclose what that thing *is*. "What is this? We answer, It is a lion, a donkey, etc. – [namely] it is. Thus it is not merely something yellow, having feet, etc., something on its own, [existing] independently. Rather, it is a *name,* a sound made by my voice, something entirely different from what it is in being looked at – and this [as named] is its true *being.* [We might say:] This is only its *name,* the thing itself is something different; but then we fall back onto the sensory representation. Or [we might say:] It is *only* a name, in a higher sense, since to begin with, the name is itself only the very superficial *spiritual being.* By means of the name, however, the object has been born out of the I [and has emerged] as *being (seyend).* This is the primal creativity exercised by Spirit. Adam gave a name to all things. This is the sovereign right [of Spirit], its primal taking-possession of all nature – or the creation of nature out of Spirit [itself]." The corollary of this statement of Hegel's in our context is that the psychotherapist's saying "I" on behalf of the patient is also his being Adam, the giver of names, on his behalf. The Hegel quote is from his "Jena Lectures: The Philosophy of Spirit (1805-6) Part I: 'Spirit according to its Concept'." https://www.marxists.org/reference/archive/hegel/works/jl/ch01a.htm (accessed 21 December 2022).

INDEX

J

ABOUT THE AUTHOR

Greg Mogenson is a registered psychotherapist and Jungian psychoanalyst practicing in London, Ontario, Canada. He is a founding member and former Vice-President of The International Society for Psychology as the Discipline of Interiority. The author of numerous articles in the field of analytical psychology, his books include *Psychology's Dream of the Courtroom*; *A Most Accursed Religion: When a Trauma becomes God*; *Greeting the Angels: An Imaginal View of the Mourning Process*; *The Dove in the Consulting Room: Hysteria and the Anima in Bollas and Jung*; *Northern Gnosis: Thor, Baldr, and the Volsungs in the Thought of Freud and Jung*, and (with W. Giegerich and D. L. Miller) *Dialectics & Analytical Psychology: The El Capitan Canyon Seminar*. He is also the author of four other essays in the ISPDI Monograph Series, *Dereliction of Duty and the Rise of Psychology, as Reflected in the "Case" of Conrad's Lord Jim*; *That Glimpse of Truth for which you had Forgotten to Ask*; *Jungian Analysis Post Mortem Dei*; and *Inwardizing Rilke's Dog of Divine Inseeing into Itself*.

For further information, visit the website at: www.gregmogenson.com

THE INTERNATIONAL SOCIETY FOR PSYCHOLOGY
AS THE DISCIPLINE OF INTERIORITY
MONOGRAPH SERIES

Other Titles in the Series

For more information about this society and
its monograph series visit the website at:
www.ispdi.org

Related Titles from Dusk Owl Books

Wolfgang Giegerich, *The Historical Emergence of the I: Essays about One Chapter in the History of the Soul.*

Wolfgang Giegerich, *What are the Factors that Heal?*

www.duskowlbooks.com

www.ingramcontent.com/pod-product-compliance
Lightning Source LLC
Chambersburg PA
CBHW031435270326

41930CB00007B/721